RED-HAIRED ANDROID

JEREMY REED

CITY LIGHTS

SAN FRANCISCO

RED-HAIRED ANDROID
© 1992 by Jeremy Reed
First City Lights Edition

Cover Photograph of Jeremy Reed by John Robinson
Cover design: John Miller, Big Fish Books

Library of Congress Cataloging-in-Publication Data

Reed, Jeremy.
  Red-haired android / by Jeremy Reed.
       p. cm.
   ISBN 0-87286-283-6 : $12.95
   I. Title.
PR6068.E34R4   1993
821 .914--dc20   93-5564

City Lights Books are available to bookstores through our primary distributor: Subterranean
Company. P. O. Box 160, 265 S. 5th St., Monroe, OR 97456. 503-847-5274. Toll-free
orders 800-274-7826. FAX 503-847-6018. Our books are also available through library
jobbers and regional distributors. For personal orders and catalogs, please write to
City Lights Books, 261 Columbus Avenue, San Francisco CA 94133.

CITY LIGHTS BOOKS are edited by Lawrence Ferlinghetti and Nancy J. Peters and
published at the City Lights Bookstore, 261 Columbus Avenue, San Francisco, CA 94133.

For Pascale

Acknowledgements are due to the following:

Lovely Jobly, The Observer, Lust, Buried Alive, Poetry Review, Owl, The Rialto, Temenos, Sphinx, Enitharmon Press, Poetry Durham, Tenth Muse, Wordlinks, Slow Dancer.

The author would like to thank the Royal Literary Fund and the Ingram Merrill Foundation for making the writing of this book possible.

He whose face gives no light,
shall never become a star.
                    William Blake

Ashes to ashes fun to funky,
we know Major Tom's a junkie.
Strung out in heaven's high,
hitting an all time low.
                    David Bowie

CONTENTS

Aliens

Earthed

Angular

Running Wild

Visuals

Erotica

Through and Out

Return of the Aliens

ALIENS

ALIENS

We're a used-up species; we wait the new
arrivals; programmed to the robotic,
De Chirico's mannequins, silver-blue

ovoid automatons buzzing the screen
as planetary invaders, gold androids
we've come to contemplate with a serene

indifference, humanoids from the stars;
yet it's in us the alien exists,
those who are less at home here than on Mars,

all trans-creatures, the androgyne, the face
in which the gender-split is healed, the eyes
containing in them, deep reaches of space,

the left and right profiles just marginally
balancing opposites as in a mask,
the lips sensuous, make-up liberally

suggestive, a nose from Donatello.
And we are here; an underground culture
who recognize our own; we always show

at times of change; music, street-fashion, art,
the mutants in ascendant, looking out
to risk a race and not an offstage-part,

a whole awareness we can get it right,
no domination. Here a boy and girl
in gold and silver, join hands in the light.

THE MAN WHO GAVE BIRTH TO HIMSELF

The wait is over: he is someone new.
The earth he'd conceived as conical, blue,

viewed from a point in space is there at last.
He remembers the robotic self-cast

he'd blueprinted, a hologrammic man;
and without knowing it he was the plan

he'd invented, consciousness grown to be
the colour of its dream, and memory

sure of its origins. He'd come to find
the particles he'd structured for the mind

were deathless molecules. The other ten
on the assemblage-point were flashback-men

inheriting faults from remembered lives,
the inner fracture that never survives

its failure. They would die again, while he
raided their input for a chemistry

to edit right for others. Who would know
he'd infiltrated, for he would outgrow

each generation, keeping just ahead
of the age increase, he who kept a red

spacecraft for private use, and would one day
create his split-off in a lunar bay.

STARDUST

Her child's called Stardust. He's detachable
from his environment: a frequency
transmitted to his cells and he's able

to bilocate. Sometimes he'll be inside
playing with a toy robot, and she'll think
it's more instructive for him if I hide

and watch him dramatize his other life;
the one in which his face is solarized
and he's married to an astronaut wife,

and it's reality, his different speech,
his eyes changing colour from blue to gold,
the easy way in which he's learnt to reach

economy of argument; no hands
or volubility. Then he moon-walks,
his movements slow as though churning up sands

the wind has drifted on a beach. She turns
volume control and watches him re-earth,
and there's no split. The little that she learns

about his double role she has to keep
suspended, blueprint it in a novel
she dreams of writing. Even deep in sleep

he has an eye open, a direct ray
focused on something that he won't let go
and shines clear as a diamond in the day.

CRYONICS

He scans a blueprint on the drawing-board,
then redirects his eyes towards the doll
who stands on guard all night, all day,
her painted eyelids closed, their gold and black
gradations emphasized, and at his touch
unlidded to a violet-blue.

His diagram connects with DNA.
It's 2,085 and the wind
is still the wind, the rain the rain and where
consciousness expands the alternatives
to living are so many, freeze-comas
that facilitate cryonic repair –
you disappear for years
and reappear
without the knowledge of a transition.
The stars from the last century are there.

He looks out of his glass-built penthouse cube
at absence; figures in oxygen masks
are working on a scaffolding.
Something's gained and something lost.
The moon-shaped bank rises over the cenotaph
on which a model astronaut
holds a miniature of the earth.
He checks the temperature gauge; his girlfriend
has been under ice for six months.
The doll looks on. She wears a wedding ring.

THE BLUE HOTEL

We take quiet refuge there on rainy days.
The rooms are blue, cobalt and deep turquoise,
and sometimes pre-recorded music plays –

Heartbreak Hotel or Famous Blue Raincoat –
Leonard Cohen's Clinton Street elegy.
The solitude surrounds us like a moat.

Above the porter's desk, I see it still,
hangs Gabriele Munter's Blaue Reiter friends,
the two reclining, while a dark blue hill

stands back from homogenous green grass.
The keys are all taken; no one goes out.
A central bullet hole has starred the glass

in a gilt mirror. A pink Cadillac
sits outside as the hotel's limousine.
We only ever see the chauffeur's back.

The maids wear blue suede shoes. Each day we find
red and white tulips arranged in a vase,
a neat ribbon-bow attached to the blind.

The place is in a forgotten quarter;
no cafés: warehouses, a cemetery.
We have novels and a tape recorder.

We're mostly silent. Punctually at eight
a blue rain falls; the singer's voice intrudes,
the old familiar 'Songs of Love and Hate'.

MADONNA

It's all a question of identity,
someone is lost inside the mutations,
the years which happen fast, schematically,
the boy-toy cat in jeans and cap

growing to be a Monroe look-alike,
blonde hair falling as though blown by the wind
emphasizing whatever facial plane
is explored from behind a mike

or angled for the lens, paparazzi
hassling for every off-mood shot –
the smudged lipstick or baggy overcoat,
the private person eating green pasta

in a small restaurant, feeling for space
after the provocation, topless thrust,
the body a sequined snakeskin
transmitting white heat, an electric lust

wired to the music. And behind the face
is the new one awaiting invention;
Madonna in orange velvet leggings
dropping popcorn nuggets into her bra

at business meetings and retrieving them,
her tongue a corolla between red lips.
It's the emptiness of being a star,
the dehumanized ennui has her change

persona, image. She would like to be
both sexes: gay-male's her alter-ego,
experience every kind of orgasm;
but now, just stares out at the New York snow

from a dark blue couch, relaxes her curves
after the gym work-out, the jacuzzi,
and wishes she was a snowballing child
whacking impacted ice at a dumb tree.

WORLD LEADERS

He enters by the backdoor: a green light
picks out the four, conspiratorially
gathered together, slumped in leather chairs.
The security are smashed on cocaine;

the dominant one whose pedantic lead
is paid lip service to by the others,
his jowls resemble a Bacon portrait –
a half melon shaped side of meat

in which the nose is blue, the eyes bright red,
has the adipose bulk of a statue
on a red carpeted plinth. He swash-rolls
like a beached whale. His wife's in bed

with an inflatable stud-doll.
The other three are parasitical
tycoon-fleas; climacteric, burning out
on uppers, snappy with their echelons

of minions. They're discussing a world coup.
The fat one talks about his impotence;
ingenious prosthetics. When he shouts
he's really laughing. Nations disappear

like that. He prefers their absence,
the black shaded areas on the map.
He proposes a nuclear canton;
depleted resources feeding one state.

They haven't noticed the one who's slipped in,
the intruder riffling through a valise.
He mounts the fat one's wife. She doesn't know
he's human, but she likes to please.

It's dark outside; the stars have gone;
the house might have been painted by Magritte.
The three get up, the fourth stays down.
He feels the bullet, but he wants to eat.

REACH FOR THE STARS

The isolation frames him in a cube.
He's like an astronaut who can't adjust
to close dimensions after seeing earth
from a near planet. He is further out
than most, and closer to reality
as he resolves it. He drives round all day
widening his radius from the city,
his silver framed shades cutting out the glare
from a cloudless sky that's part green, part red,
with artificial hills backdropped
as screen props in the landscaping.
The road is true, its metal hurts his head.

He feeds cassettes into the cartridge-slot
or lets the silence blow in through windows
and settle as a sort of company
lighting his nerves. He thinks into absence.
Occasionally a goat will trot
across the highway, or a science-fiction junky
wave from his own miniature launching-site
at the by now familiar gold car,
the dust behind it, a blonde smoking wave.
Today he looks for hitch-hikers –
a girl in silver jeans with silver hair
accommodates. Her bra is two black stars.
She fills a space. They stop at a motel.
The light falls one side green and one side red
over the rocket-shaped air-cushioned bed.

RED-HAIRED ANDROID

The red-haired android delivered from space
worked as a cabaret act, drove a car
panelled from a crashed Boeing's fuselage
and on the silver bonnet a red star

suggested origins. Always alone,
shooting film with the inquisitive need
to find the odd in the familiar,
he remained isolated, then a clone

hung round his dressing-room, would never speak,
but followed, blank-eyed, obsessed, dead to all
around him – concentrated on the way
the other moved and spoke, as though a leak

informed him of a mutual energy.
The two grew indivisible; the first
graduated from cabaret to pop,
his light-show so spectacular they thought

that it would blind. He rented for himself
a whole apartment block and moved about
from floor to floor behind black shaded glass.
The other slept out in an army truck

he'd ransacked from the lost revolution
and painted zany orange. Bullet holes
peppered the windshield. For the spectator
the two were interchangeable in roles

and daring; challenging society
by living outside it. The show went on,
bringing with it a greater privacy
as fame advanced, and a controversy

that brought the cameras up close to find out
the absence of a biochemistry
relatable to earth, and the next act
would prepare the way for their own species.

ORANGE HANDS, YELLOW HANDS

Three girls in silver enter to my right
and are conspicuous infiltrators.
They check miniature screens and a blue light

shows their instructor. They type in a code
with an orange hand, cancel with yellow.
Their planet's on call, and a quarried road

blasted through glass mountains flicks up on view.
We've come to accept them. Always women
banded in threes, they represent the new

we haven't reached. They take high apartments
and put in shaded windows, buy up all
our latex jumpsuits, shades, skin nutrients,

and won't assimilate with us. Their speed
is a corrective to our lethargy;
they overtake rather than state a need,

and seem to want of our environment,
something of which we're unaware. We read
in their behaviour the presentiment

we are deletable. Their leader's here
in the form of a sculpture; but she's masked.
They're waiting for her and she will appear.

Another three arrive in this small bar.
We'd like to speak to them, but they're watching
whatever happens back home on their star.

ARRIVALS

We stand or sit and hear the tannoy blur
correcting errors. There's a bluish light
clips in from outside, and the faces run
together. At times it seems we're in flight,

expected soon where we break nails for those
who haven't touched down yet. Their time and ours
won't synchronize. We hear a jet blast off;
take its reverberations. It is hours

we've lived and waited, and security
keep infiltrating. Someone brings me here,
and there are other arrivals who might
break through the barrier and disappear . . .

I'm afraid my dead father will return
in another incarnation. He'll be
a youth or student on language exchange.
'It's your turn next', he'll say, dismissively,

and I'll follow his back out of the hall.
I watch the new ones come through. Some are tanned
and wear dark glasses. An Italian girl
trails a red scarf. He's waiting there as planned,

and they're united. It is getting late
and there is no announcement of delay
or redirected routes; and if I missed
the information or got the wrong day,

it's due to displacement, expecting more
than will ever occur, a silver face
materialized to greet me as a visitor
come through the doors and from the back of space.

MOON-TANNING

She slips into a silver bikini
on warm nights and feels the moonshine
polish to a cool tan

a blue luminosity on her skin
that's travelled as reflected light
so far she has to think of it
as a near mirror, and she bares her breasts

by day so absorbent of sun
to feel them touched silver
radiant areolas

a surf-line off in the distance
minting a shine out of the dark
Aegean

She is quite naked now receiving light
on a blue towel and turns over
as though for a lover

Later she'll go back in, draw the curtains
to emphasize her body's glow
slip into bed and feel his force

create a fluent pearl in her

DREAM CAMERAMAN

At night the films I watch diversify;
if the cameraman's there, he's out of sight,
the sequence breaks so often, fast cut-ups
in which I'm vulnerable, a flick of light
and I am standing on a pyramid
observing a sun with a skyscraper
burning in its centre; white, orange, black,
the colours change: it is my father now,
grown younger in death who tries to reach me
across a fast flowing river.
I wave to him through dream-semiotics.
I wasn't born when he had such blond hair,
such unstrained features. The river runs on.

All day I brief myself to catch the man
who shoots imaginative montage.
I grow obsessed I've seen him half turn round,
present a profile with closed eyes,
a black jumper. He has no hair. And hides.
Tonight I could be taken anywhere;
I fly or travel at great speed
and when the journey's too bumpy I wake
with flashbacks fizzing into a vortex.
I catch at symbols: blood, an outbuilding
in which the dark was manual,
fire-stairs zigzagging towards high blue skies,
this time a girl I knew floats out in space,
I can't reach or detain her.
I'm no nearer to the source; he's incognito,
angling shots from impossible storeys.
I'll meet him one day, running at the lens,
he cutting the film, so I'll never know . . .

IMPROVISATIONS

We're astronauts, we've moved away from earth
and grown dissociated from bodies:
I saw myself ten years ago, a man
in touch, wanting a man or a woman,

nerves burning to undress her with my teeth.
We're on screen as the new species,
surprised at the belief we're still human,
or are the programmes brought from the archives,
suggesting we were here
and now we're gone into another dimension?

Ten digits and Dashmael has oral sex
from Cindy by suggestive instruction.
His ear's the receiver, the perfect fit
for a taped message. She's the exhibit

he imagines as a sexless android.
We're somewhere else. The planetarium's
our nearer shore. I'm dressed, my silver boots
and suit don't match the street.
I step between two television screens.
Mars shows up with its dust fall-out,
and I am there by thinking myself there.
Later the shuttle. Strange lives on the moon.
He tells me how he has sex back on earth.
His video-wife has twice given birth.

AFTER THE GREAT DISCOVERIES

After the great discoveries the maps
were altered, what was land was sea,
and what was sea became deserts, plateaus,
stone forests. A red bird flew in the sky
announcing changes. Where is Nebraska?
the white-suited American
released his Cadillac's shaded window,
and we indicated back somewhere, anywhere
across a savanna to the ocean.
Coral trees with seashells for fruits
were incongruous visuals on the road
that led to the expatriate café –
a resurrected Dallas hall,
a singer smooching over a piano,
improvising without a memory.
The patrons talked of Nisir, Ararat,
the lost sanctuaries, mountains under sea,
and of reversion, things stood upside down
might rectify. It's all illusory . . .

Outside the air was so intensely blue
it powdered the road with crystals. We drove
in no direction. In the displacement,
sharks, whales, dolphins had died stranded and showed
as roadside monuments. We drove to keep
ourselves from entering a sleep
in which we hallucinated. Times Square
was sapphire; fish flickered through the subway.
We tuned in to our radio
and heard Sinatra singing from some town
they were still building, 'Hey sunshine,
the blue blue water keeps on coming down.'

WE'RE LEAVING YOU

A twist of orange and the sky's on fire.
They've left their canoe on the coral sand

and walk towards the shore. He's Japanese,
and she American. She wears
a stars and stripes T-shirt, bleached jeans,
and he a combat jacket. Dungarees.
They've come from somewhere. Another island?

A white boundary wall runs around the coast.
They read the red graffiti arabesques:
The New World's On The Other Side.
No one bribes the cosmonauts.

They stand suspended as a guard takes up
position on the wall. A mongoloid child,
he views the beach, takes out a knife
and shaves a driftwood stave.
He cuts the crosspiece for his apple's grave.
And other children suddenly appear
along the wall; casual, yelping like dogs,
they fail to monitor the beach
with military vigilance.

The couple back off, light a fire
and cook the fish that he's harpooned.
They'll have to turn back, but they stay
and watch pink clouds shot peach above the bay.

She takes her baby out of the canoe,
wraps it, and leaves it to propitiate
the cosmonauts. She sings 'we're leaving you.'
He cuts rapid strokes through the blue.

PINK SHERBET

It's snowing on the Russian beach,
the Moscow blonde, a Monroe look-alike
poses for the camera, her one pink strand
is flamingo, a reddened drinking straw
hung vertical. Why not read Mandelshtam
by the Black Sea? but this is pop –
sixties music for the nineties –
trans-siberian psychedelia –

poetry readings in the sky.
She's naked beneath a fur coat
except for sheer stockinged legs, a black film
between her and the snow.
The Russian pop group on the radio
beside her are somewhere in space.

She puts on dark glasses against the glare.
We watch the untelevised demo.
'I want pink sherbet in Estonian snow'

the English band play. And it starts to snow.

LOST DAUGHTERS OF THE ASTRONAUT

And who they are and how they went away
and where : a bonfire on the beach
billows a wick of blackish smoke. A skinny boy
looking for someone, draws her in the sand:
a pictograph on a gold tabula rasa.
He met her here a year ago and lost
interest in her third dimension.
She'd driven for so long she couldn't understand
a road stays still despite the rotation
that slips beneath us unnoticed. Red hair,
a lip-burn, a cyborg logo
on a denim shoulder, a sister back somewhere;
the skinny boy spitting blue mackerel on the fire
remembers how when he'd made love to her
he seemed to enter space, her momentum
stretched him to vertigo; he saw the stars
packed with energy in his head.
He woke to find her gone, a photograph wallet
dropped in the sand. 'Marylou snapping me
in the process . . .' the date and time,
the location, Cape Kennedy.

And Marylou who turned up here one day,
dark haired, formidable, was on the road
to find her sister; her father
had entered solar time. She swam naked
and opened her legs to the sun. It was a ritual.
Now shredding flesh from the fish skeleton,
the boy's thankful for the deserted beach.
The sea brings news of the world. There's a child
around the headland whom he likes to teach.

OUR TIME

It is so much our own, we misconstrue
the meaning of our being here.
That barbecue by a moon-dusted lake,
diffused pearl brightening, that midnight swim

and later still, a roof-garden party;
events we lived through – were they part of us?
or a red dye tinting blue memory.
Sometimes the smallest thing, a terminus,

a filling station on a stretch of road
remembered for its poplars; a record
of the moment filling the afternoon
gives us a sense of time, we have arrived

at a point in the journey, but can't stay.
And if we turned round seeking to reverse
our notion of non-fixity, we'd meet
no memoranda, only the same road,

the city that we'd left behind, its signs
pointing to the centre, our work, our friends,
our nervousness in hoping we'll outlive
all other generations, deathless ones

brought out to sit on the edge of the world?
waiting with prayer beads and bowls filled with rain.
The immediate falls as a tree-curtain,
we have to imagine the other side

of a dark forest. So many stopped here.
Their footprints are erased and ours are new.
We have to go on; feed fuel to the car.
The sky from here to there is prussian-blue.

LIFE BEYOND MARS

The one who's been there, keeps his back to us,
and drinks in a bar close to the airfield,
windy buffetings on a blue plateau
fenced from civilians, a convex hole
punched through the air's like a shattered ceiling.
His silver leather jacket, collar up
to hide his nape, brushes with silver hair
worn in a plait. He seems to stare
into the great spaces he's left behind,
and is withdrawn, unreachable.

Ballistic experts, test pilots,
a transsexual barman who flutters eyes
made up like peacock butterflies,
the bar's a relaxant, and synthesizer waves
invoke spatial atmospherics.
                                        The crowd
gathers each night from curiosity
and leaves without ever seeing the face
they have to construct imaginatively.
A robot, mutant, or someone transformed
so finally they are surgical skin;
glass eyes, so many physical anomalies?
He sits in a private recess
and never moves. The barman's cocktail dress
is sewn with stars. The two might be lovers?

He's grown to be an exhibit.
A focal point like a painting
we've learnt to treat familiarly.
If he turned round it might deflate our dream.

Occasionally we hear him scream.

THE COLBRIGHT SCENARIO

The trial rehearsals can't resolve the scene.
On lunar sands a silver parasol's
fixed on the beach, and sheltered from the glare
a mutant lies beside the recorder
that feeds him planetary data. They're off somewhere
in deeper space, the androids who elect
to search for other colonies. A green,
a purple, a red sun triple above
a landscape without fixtures. Compact glass.
When music sounds it is Jim Morrison's
'Break on Through to the Other Side',
leading and phased out periodically,
before the screen jumps with flashbacks,
the singer's death, lunar shots of our earth,
a blue egg in the blue vacuum. The ones
who live down there have moved into the hills,
the mountains, but the change goes on:
they set up fires to attract UFOs, craft
that cluster now they're visible. Ninety
outside, and Colbright retires to the shade.
They know him in this café opposite
the studio; he smokes cigars,
caresses his one rounded female breast,
and writes his findings on the hidden stars.

DUSTING THE ARM-REST

Poetry is a wolf watching the world,
feral dog-eyes yellowing in the night,
coming at things from wild interiors,
uncompromising where it kills;

always a ranging outsider.
A child, a wolf came to me in a dream
and made to leap. The hands I raised
to ward it off were written on with words.

Poetry sleeps too often, tries to beg
acceptance with the complacent.
It's closer to the street-corner, the edge,
the solitary who arrive without precedent –

Blake, Rimbaud, the distraught Artaud,
the hallucinated, the criminal,
the one standing with his back to the wall,
defiant, while the rain blows in.

The wolf is restless, drops down from the hills
to browse amongst parked cars. It's everywhere;
its bolt announcing change, smashing a hole
through ideologies, leaving its mark

on the blue day. A winter's night, a moon
pointing a glacial brushstroke.
There's revolution in the agonized
twisting of a shriek into words.

Lean, angry, unshakeably polarized,
the night-intruder's there to hit its mark,
imparting a savage dementia
to the one waiting for it in the dark.

YOU WERE WEARING BLACK

In the dead of winter; one hand
on the fridge, an orange sun streaming through
the window from the bright ice-day.
Your life in ruin or in dread;
but no, the car is parked outside, your skirt
invites the eye to drop dramatically,
vertically, then re-climb, back to your belt-pin's
oval. And your girlfriend waits outside,
a cigarette reddening in her lips,
her frosty silence, absolute. The dare
not cooling. *This is love.*

You rehearse what you'll say to your husband,
his frightened mannerisms depicting
the expectation of a man who knows
the worst; someone who swallows his own vertigo
into the down-drop. He is like vodka
poured into a panopticon of ice.
He won't come back at you, wounded lion
excelling in his guillotine
hang-ups in business: a dead telephone.
You're dressed for his return: an end to things.
Your hand glitter is different: it's her gift.
An extravagant galaxy of rings.

NEW YEAR'S EVE

There's a door left open;
the one I never took
from here to there with the expectation
missed promises in retrospect afford.
No footprints anywhere, I look
around, the yellow wash
of headlights stripe a fox sneaking away,
red coat and heavy brush
finding a bolthole in the dark.

Presentiment has had me stop the car,
and overhead a cloud delays
as though it's found me out. Its volute stays.
I notice in the lights a book,
a passport, photograph, and are they mine?
I've seen them somewhere, their identity
is owned to by my memory.
And shards of glass dazzle the road,
the jigsaw fragments of an accident?
I search my face, my hands for blood.
The frost has brushed glitter into the mud.

The door's ajar and a white light
spills to a trapezoid on the threshold.
I keep thinking if I can get inside
my senses will regain the clarity
to know the reason for my being here.
The cloud is closer; it's above my head
and reddening. My breath's a question mark
in the crystal, partying air.
I stand outside the door, but nothing's clear.

DETOXIFICATION

So help me purify,
whatever new cells will regenerate
my clean blood at the end of it,
the cellular need no longer this desperate
fight in the dark hours to get free
of the cycle's remorseless continuity,
the chemical's biography
controlling mine. We're a duality,
old partners in this game of high and low
and more latterly
as cross-currents in a whirlpool.

The pain's inhuman. When I breathe
sand pours into my mouth, my nerves are stretched
along the white line of a road
over which humming cars explode
in red flashes. I've lost a skin,
an onion peeled to the interior,
and things move in –
faces that threaten, voices amplified,
an army kicking through a shell-gapped house.

I break my trust and recourse to the drug,
promising it's the final one
before I kick the habit, and succumb
to quiet, the torn skin knits back,
and faithfully ascendant, it rises,
my black inner chemical sun.

WHERE WE ARE NOW

I check the street. It is a foreign place.
A red-haired hooker links arms with a priest
and disappears. The crowds are out of town
parked in their bannered cars, waiting for Vince
to show, preceded by a slow cortege,
black limousines conveying the old powers
towards a wasteland burial.
The waiting cars are dressed in silk streamers –
a violent clash of blue and red and white.
The morning brightens after thunder showers.

I thought of Vince and his five years away,
his hairdressing salon in a complex
I couldn't find. I remembered him blond,
magnetic in his attraction,
too thin, too intense, he was burning out
in a small town. His two wives, two husbands
had fought publicly in the street.
After the cure he'd gone away.
We heard of him living at Black Rock Sands,
reformed and teaching. The escalation
was sudden, and this bulldozed gap
under conversion was his studio.

I walk the changed perspective of the town.
I'll drive away before helicopters
unleash gold balloons, red carnations.
An army of street thugs look like opposition.
Crop-skulled delinquents, they're on every street,
dressed in combat clothes. Vince will be here soon.
After the rain, we settle to the heat.

EARTHED

OUR TIME

It's blues. A buried jazz that leads the way
impromptu, catching us out in the street
as though a wave delivered a conch shell
right at our feet in the run-back of surf.
There is a way of knowing who we are
by what we do, the rest is too close up
to evaluate. If I could turn back
I'd find no clearer meaning than today;
the girls with red hennaed hair in this club,
the ones in black leather shorts and thigh-boots
are marked by an image they'll remember
as theirs, and was that ever us?
We're ejected like a pilot's black box
after the crash into another age,
marram grass building high above the dunes.

But now we run direct into the screen,
not extras but participants, alive
to how we'll change the world and not be changed
by the intention. And it's jazz pursues
our melody, directing each towards
his thrilling awareness that *now* means *here* –
the gold light in the heart of a forest,
the empty turtle shell found on the beach,
a first adventurous kiss leading to
impossible surprise, a rounding out
of sensory confusions. Let me reach
your centre and in going there
discover timelessness, the blue interior
of underwater caves, and coming out
the light of our own century
there for the living. Absolutely free.

HALF WAY

Red roses tumble into the poem
whenever I imagine Hölderlin's
breaking point: his Hälfte Des Lebens,

the midway step suspended on a bridge,
no going back as the planks fall away
to weathered driftwood in the stream.
Autumn a red leaf caught in a sunbeam.

Behind our shoulder the landscape is stone
or flaming woods. Water won't cool
grained contours on the hands,
a map of travel realized
in work-lines, things half done.

The break in continuity
is like two nerves no longer connecting;
the current forks into a V
navigated by a black,
a white swan.

The rift instructs that there's no turning back.
The sun is warm and yellow pears
are lanterns hung above the track.

MY FATHER'S PEN

The space you would have occupied
is someone else's. A face in the crowd
seen through the cinematic frame
of this café window – it's almost you,
the green clothes and fair hair the same,

you might never have gone away
and it's me who is looking out
from a displaced dimension on this day,
writing with your turquoise Parker,
the nib's individual temper

more yours than mine; the one heirloom
I've made my own, emerald ink
replacing your blue residue,
your baroque flourishes toned down
to my rounder, less dramatic

legibility. Pen and paper –
my symbiotic drug; for you
the instrument meant books, ledgers,
inveterate routine. Outside
the scene changes, a windy blue

sky's cloud flotillas build to rain.
Couples pick up speed on the run,
a blond boy and a pink-haired girl
are touched by intermittent sun
continuing through the fast shower.

This street was part of your daily
itinerary. I look again,
half expecting to see you pass.
Diamond hexagonals spot on
to tadpoles silvering the glass.

I've claimed this pen to write the books
you wouldn't have read. We were far.
Your blood, my ink, a tightening
that precedes words, and now the light
breaks on the window like a star.

MARTINS

for Pascale

Shrill interjections at twilight
up there in the pointillistic crazing
of aerial plankton,
jamming on insect-glitter,
they are to the ear and eye an alert
to the day's passing, a blue scud
shot through by their zigzag curvatures,
black arrows planing on a trajectory

of thermals, screaming low over rooftops,
filling me in with the expectancy
of their buzzing dynamics,
their unfaltering manoeuvres,
their drift-and-dart pressure
punctuated by drops
out of focus, uptake and climb

in weird geometric abstractions.
To you they are elegiac,
recalling summer evenings outside,
a grandmother dead
who shared your awakenings; light of hers
lives on in your stories.

I go outside from my typing;
the sky's blue translucency
is sharp with their cries, their pointed flicker
towards homing; the sun's red hoop
catching their fast, frenetic loop,
and the trees massive, black, as though mourning.

STILL

At the year's end a continuity;
the generosity of stars, I count and name
the constellations. Old night, new night, gone.

The doorframe that I stand against peels paint.
Words go like that into decay,
what books will cross to another century,
be ploughed into steel earth. And rise again?

We carry things forward so far.
Our lives are fragile. What will hold
at breaking point? My mind, my hands.
The earth or us?

An owl is hunting in the dark;
quick thing, its feathers grained like bark,
bib wet with blood.

The night shows star-antlers above the wood.

KEEPERS OF THE NIGHT

I bring them stories to propitiate
their watchful eyes. And we are so many
who take our allegories to a place
heaped with dead birds and multi-national flags,
a burnt piano, the life-size mannequins
of tyrants, dictators, universal
agents of ruin. Smoke drifts into space
above that threshold, and the keepers stay
like guards we never see. We know they're there,
and still demand we bring the old story
of life and loss to them; the warped spiral
of all our inconsistencies, the thread
that snaps while we approve its right tension,
the things that happen and seem without cause,
but alter us. They're not indifferent:

they seem to say the clue is in the tale,
but we can't find it or have forgotten
the meaning. We've left it to drown
like a white horse trapped in a quarry pool;
we thought it was an hour ago
it went missing, but it is years. The days
are like that, stabilizing round the night
when we elucidate the happenings
that take us to the edge of a city
so many wars have passed through. It is dark:
I've made the journey in a century
that's part of time. White ashes dust the air.
I hear a voice say, 'tell me if you dare . . .'

WRITING MY BIOGRAPHY

I miss so much of what's happening to me
that I'm the other. Yesterday we met
and thought how much has been aleatory,
just given on the chance like a sunbeam
surprising by its blue and red smoky
arrival on the page. We're reconciled
on better days, at moments in the street
when we agree it's worthwhile going on
to claim the meaning chalked up by a dream
as it intersects with reality.
Last week the face that came at me through smoke
and rubble in natural scenic colour –
my house was smashed by looting troops, was there
the other day in a crowd flash,

I recognized him; now he's gone again.
We're constantly surprised, this me and you
and not much wiser as to why we're here,
and that we share a secrecy
in what we're doing. We are really two,
the actor and the spectator
and the gap never narrows. Just turn round,
the other says: what do you remember
with authenticity; an autumn day
in a red blowy October,
faces of lovers, friends and incidents
which retain clarity? They're like fall-out
from a near planet; bitty, fractured stuff.
And what most stays is like a gold leaf stuck
to the road surface, then the foot,
something that clings because it is misplaced,
yet still gives intimations of a root.

SHOOTING A POP VIDEO

The weird perspective's created by props,
a massive cupola-shaped chandelier
is let down from the ceiling. Mannequins
are placed like birthday candles round the edge,
each with a cigarette angled
from scarlet lips; and the mime-dancer stops,

amazed at finding his transvestite's face
copied in each cloned mannequin.
He lights a cigarette and stands stock-still;
it's like he's being hunted by guitars
which enter spookily, laid back
reverberations, hesitant, a ricochet
dispersed by echo-chambers, returning
with a vehemence which might kill;
a massive wall of sound across which stars
explode in maniacal reds and blues.
The dancer appeals to the twenty clones,
and each responds with a bright splinter-tear,
his vocals introducing Jacqueline,
half of whose face divides each mannequin.
She is the sultry one he met by chance
on a deserted beach. Her hair's so black
it is a thunderstorm. Now full facial,
she's everywhere looking at him,
her body moulded into black sequins,

but he can't claim her. She is blown away
and the guitars continue their attack.

ADVANCES

The sea makes big advances, white on blue
arrivals from the universal momentum.
She thinks silence and listens to Mompou.
Hang-gliders dragonfly across the bay.

Her lover wants a tight black cocktail dress,
tarted couture, her femininity
pronounced right down to red painted toenails.
She smokes; the other stares straight out to sea.

What brought them to the coast has kept them there.
A man was involved and the tearing free,
squally, masochistic, lasted a year.
He wrecked his car, its jagged metal

still rips defiantly
at her present. Occasionally it comes between
them and they drink. A little dab of green
tinctures their lives with jealousy.

They rarely entertain. Friends from Paris
come once a year; a Gertrude Stein
look-alike with cropped bluish hair.
A stringy girl who dresses as a boy.

They watch the beach arrivals start to swarm.
They kiss slowly in the window.
It is their way, hoping a peeping-tom
might watch them naked as they start to flow.

WITH HORSES

If I could, in this big disarming wind
slicing the thermals, shredding stencilled leaves
into a swirl, I'd take shelter
with white horses, nervous horses
got in under thinning oaks at the edge
of a leaf-flapping meadow – amber and green
                                  and gold,
and smelling of earth spices – black ginger
pine and saffron brought by the sea
shouldering its equinoctial spray
on to blue beaches and wild with white horses
cresting the surf as it curves
to fall over the world. And the rain
as it cools my face, impacted, spotting
out of the leaf-storm would have the horses fidget,
standing the wind, jittery, overwired,
shifting as though choreographing a journey
with each precise alteration
of stance, each electric nerve-message.
Leaves falling like stars from the flying sky.

I would be there in that field I've known since
childhood,
a place instructive to the lyric, words
constellating round the inner
landscape exchanged for the one outside,
with space expanding in my head
to grasslands, unobstructed pampas live
with horses under green sky-plains,
and now in the blustery open day,
not being there, I have to travel by
fluent recall to a reality
of horses, wind, gold leaves, a shrieking jay.

JAYS

The sky opens in the wing's feathering –
an azure rift accordioned into black
and white as the pinions disclose.

The idea of the bird in mental space:
it was blue all over,
vulnerably bright, then chestnut and rose
above me with its survivor's primal
communicative urgency
lifted from carbonized forests.

I stood confused by the nature of reality:
the air like silk on my face,
the jay in another dimension, fixed

into codified instincts, his world more
                                        than mine,
with my inner retreat, my imagining
him as he is or not.
Autumn around; leaf-gold and rot.

I walked on with the real bird in my head,
jet eyes alert, head tilted forward, wings
fanned; agonized gutturals;

and left my imaginary jay in depleted
oak-leaves; a turquoise outsider,
eyes full of journeys, forests, extinguished planets,

conceiving how he'd alter the nature of things
through the exchange of inner and outer,
dreaming the world and finding both still there,

the lifted visual, the claw's grip on bark.

BLUE MIRAGE

for Asa Benveniste

My writing hand carries your name across
savannas of the posthumous
at camel's pace; a finger-clenched shadow
compact with language, I arrive too late

to distinguish you from the blue mirage
that travels with the poem. You are there
again at our first meeting: gelled black hair,
black shirt, thin as the nervous cigarette

you kept replacing – a stubbed hecatomb;
and I was nineteen, self-destructive, mad
with an implosive poetry
you helped me focus. I owe more to you

than any other; it's continuous,
I find you on the page I work each day,
you're in its mirror, the glass framed with black
snakes stringing at the intersection point . . .

Magician, poet, you were often sad,
distracted, silent for long intervals,
taking your divination from a book
out of which music, flowers and birds flew

in the migration that you've joined. I see
you reading the I Ching in Kentish Town,
the light in Norfolk. You were generous
beyond all asking, self-effacing, known

to those who saw through your invisibility
a poet working. Gold in the window,
Art Tatum on the stereo,
you journeying back to the Jewish kings,

your origins, and more than anything
your evaluation of the image
lives with me. It's a silent commitment
this thankless living for the word; the dust

we raise, resettles. You have gone to find
the place your poems led to. Is it far
or nearer than you thought? It's over there,
and lights are blazing on the bottom stair.

ANEMONES

They hold the mood given by a painting,
the silence too.
We can't break in nor they force out
of a pliant stemmed radius; they bend,
a snake with a mauve flower for a head,
a red, a blue. This white one is swan-necked
and enquires back into itself.
If I could see them as they are
I'd realize their movement, vibration.
They're further from me than the nearest star.

Gunpowder smudges of black seed
line a down-curled scarlet petal.
They seem to drink their colours from water
with amethyst cocktail straws.
I look around them. I am seer seen.

What if a painting became vocable?
If in Renoir's Moulin de la Galette
the couples spoke – the straw-hatted young man
making advances in the dance,
his blonde-haired partner, reciprocating.
Would we respond by listening
as a waiter brought drinks to a table.

Anemones concentrate. They're the focal point
of colour in this room. And if I look,
will I see them go mad in confinement,
rotate the vase in a circular storm
of shed petals, leaving black-buttoned stems
questioning me about this new event?

BLUEBELLS

for Jack Barker

The near patches were lavender
with blue assertive in the mauve; breezy
amongst stitchwort, and even stooping down
to pick, one had to qualify the blue
in grey and indigo.

We'd come back to learn their scent
and it was different
again, this year. A more elusive strain:
hyacinth diffused by rain.
We wouldn't let it go,
olfactory confusion, and breathed the air
as though by slow degrees made high
and getting there.

Returning here was a ritual: the good,
the bad, we brought with us was individually
modified by this place, a scrambled wood,
the grasses combed out blue,
no one around and we free to confess
our inner hopes, the buried fears
that form in us like ammonites –
negative psychic potential.

We lay back in the warm grass and the scent
arrived in catches. Nothing to cling to;
and by familiarity the woods
grew to a concentrated blue.

BLUE CORNFLOWERS

Are manganese-blue
on such raffish bushy stems, royal-blue suns
constellating by poppy,
if we look to invoke the vanishing
impressionistic cornfield. Renoir's colours, Monet.

And close up in this room they dominate.
Blues which are purpling
as the light vibrates.
I can't avoid their intimate design;
our confrontation. The blue-idea uncompromised
by blue; my visual notation.

Think of them magnified as blue cartwheels,
crowding me out of my space, so I cower
beneath their penumbra. A bluish-black.
A man in hiding from a take-over.

They look towards a racing sky;
clouds boiling off from peaks. I stand my ground.
My only weapon is my eye.

BLUE POT

Clouds and the altimetry
of their crevices; and this acacia
unloosing white flowers on a blue day
into a blue pot
positioned in the grass.

And it's a fact your oiled body's naked,
a string of pearls around your hips,
orange-tip butterflies floating the breeze.

And it's an eccentricity
this collecting the random fall
of petals in a turquoise pot.
The jade-green beeches give on to a wood.

It's chance association that our mood
elects we'll make love in the burning grass,
thresh out a crater, while a thrush looks on,

crackling amongst last year's leaf rot.

THINGS THAT STAY

A Coke can's red paint peeled to a glitter
hooked at the eye intrusively,
up on the furze, a gorse-thatched stone ruin
ledged above a blueblack sea,

was a hollow egg needled by the winds
an outcrop shell that stuck
its hobbled walls in memory,
and stayed luminous in the inner eye.

That and so many other incidents
condition how we read this world;
a white stallion head-down beneath the trees
turning to look and that stare going in

as though the roles were instantly reversed,
the horse staring out at itself through me.
Mostly they coruscate; the big, the small
upheavals which really signify.

You might be walking down an empty street
thinking of nothing but the red sunset,
when something interferes, a catch of scent,
a face you'd seen regularly of late

and half-forgotten, lets you know
you're wanted if you'll make the date.
The spontaneous that deepens is what shines,
if we think of a personal mosaic,

pink and white cherry trees blown to a froth,
a woodland path remembered in childhood,
that house, that face, a bolting fox
seen by its red brush, looking back.

PROMISED LAND

They leave the car and contemplate
how they've journeyed to the frontier.
She interlinks her arm with his.
Their actions reciprocate fear.

Heat bounces back off a metallic road
that's littered with beer bottles. On one side
the blue pines are familiar.
They've travelled through them. Now they cannot hide.

In front of them a perimeter fence
screens off a desert; and their serial card
will activate the gate. He searches out
the pink and black strip; and it admits two.

They stand and stare. Old cans rust by the wire,
and cacti show green flourishes –
a red, an orange flower.
Cinders are still hot from an extinct fire.

And is it a mirage? the white
hotel that stands situated in space,
grids over the windows, a guard
patrolling the roof. It's a trick of light.

They're apprehensive they may not return,
commitment implies an austerity
they'd not expected. A coffee machine
is on the wrong side of the gate.

They stay a long time and equivocate.
They've sold up to come to the new.
She leads him to the slot and takes the card.
Together they look back, then walk on through.

ARCHITECT

The blue light is a lake above the town
and periodically aircraft lower
into the glide-ways, punctuate the hour
as international visitants. He keeps
a watch on their traffic, imagining
the anxious faces coming down,
the cloud gaps giving on to light again
in intermittent flickers. Run-up blinds.

It's grown to be an obsession
transmitted to his working hours, the tone
and vibrational characteristics
of recognized engines. He is an architect
working at a board in a studio,
blueprinting a future geometry –
your interior as an exterior,
the archetypes, fetishes as design,
a block of flats shaped like a stiletto,
a house in the form of a cat,
the possibilities extend to the perverse
or the consolatory: he has them all.
An aircraft's shadow crosses on his wall,
something of him goes down with it,
a pleasing vertigo, a shift
in consciousness assisting the idea
which in time grows to his new exhibit.

HOUSE OF MIRRORS

It climbs back as a vertical smoke-plume,
a white waterfall's vaporous double,
and higher up a little mountain train
shows in snatches between dense conifers.
The house is somewhere. It is under rain
or clear, but we can't realize
its presence without self-identity.
I've passed it often, looking out not in
and missed the image that would see me through
to its interior. The hour speeds by,
the rapid days, the century;
the house is still there if the traveller stops

and lets the image stabilize; but where
and how is the location made,
and is there anyone inside? Perhaps
there'll be a double or an analyst,
or someone that I should have known,
but never got to, and a central room
in which to meditate; a red Rothko
prominent on one wall? I'll stay a time,
inquisitive, exploratory,
and meet in every room someone I've been,
the states of mind, the visual roles assumed,
and find my guide in the study alone,
impartial, white coated, a finger raised
to his thin lips, a file under one arm;
and there's no need to explain what you've done
he motions, pointing out to the garden,
its mirror lake, mirror trees, mirror chairs
awaiting two who'll sit and hear the train
so close, they might be on it going there.

BRILLIANCE

The poem attracts colour. It will take
a greenish-yellow from De Chirico,
a red and blue from Miró, and a mauve
from Dufy, a pink from Chagall,
and mix its palette. It's plasticity
the poet wants, and a tonality
appropriate to inner space
and those discoveries the process finds.

A single starfish on the dark-red sands,
and then a diamond chair, a black piano
to which a white dinghy is moored.
The lyric composition keeps me there,
I am expecting someone to arrive
before the picture fades. Who will it be?
And will the sea come in and lift the boat?
The angle tilts, and it's another place,
two men walk step by step into dust hills
towards a cylindrical missile-head
nose-crashed into a crater. Someone's watching them:
it is a dwarf crouched behind a cactus;
his clothes are of the subtle green
Matisse employed in painting Saint Tropez.
Green Man. Red earth. The scenic blurs again,
the poet shifts back to external things,

a little lost at street noise, light crowding
into the flat, estranged from what is there,
thinking perhaps this lamp, this furniture
have just arrived as props out of the air.

AN AFFAIR

He saw the curling wave run for the beach,
over his shoulder, as he zipped the car
up to a coastal height; the hanging reach

of surf appearing again between dunes,
its placement cadenced across burnished sand,
recalling to his mind those afternoons

years earlier, when he'd come here alone
looking for stability, something cool
rounded and permanent like the green stone

he'd pocketed as epidote and learnt
to take a different one with each visit,
smarting at how the brilliant salt grains burnt

a blood-nick in his finger, and today
he examines his trophy, a speckled
black and white granite disc grabbed from the spray

among the grating jumble. Now he waits;
her car will show at three, familiar
comfort to a passion which he debates

as bitter, sharp like the salt in his hand,
illicit, and more exciting for that.
He parks the car where a sheltered pine-stand

provides a recess. Stone by stone relate
the story of his coming here, the calms,
the sudden fears – a winter sea in spate . . .

They are a necklace. Grey, blue, green and white.
Already he can hear her car. The wind
is making big knife-slashes at the light.

BORDER COUNTRY

My map is round. First it was square, then cut
into a blue oblong. Tectonic plates
colliding, or telluric upheaval,
the big heat-flash: something made it like that.
I got my map from a reinforced hut;
a suited man who looked like Franz Kafka,
said, 'we are round, moon-white and flat,
but could revert to square or progress to oval?'
'And where's the earth?' I asked. He didn't know,
since the near planets blizzarded like snow
in a glass paperweight. This is the moon
I thought; we're the border country
to the great curve of space; the stepped back stars
have receded to still remoter points.

The notion became a reality.
I looked for signs left by Apollo II,
junked missile casings, orbital debris,
and walked around what looked like a black sea,
vitreous, immobile and very dark.
Two men in mylex-suits patrolled the beach.
A woman stood beside a silver tent.
I thought I knew her but the vertigo
of movement had me confused. I would reach
a parallel surface in time:
this white was like the centre of a disc,
the record bands separated by grooves.
And if I walked across them to the edge,
was there an exit or a sky-deep drop?
I traced my way back to the Info hut:
the man assured me he had vital news;
tomorrow we'd be oval; and today,
enjoy the last of the circular views.

ALL THE WAY DOWN

You're living where the air-waves travel, high
on music as the new language,
the lyric pick-up. It's immediacy
you live through: pop and strawberry shampoo,

white walls and aluminium
furniture awaiting mutants? The blue
afternoon's full of black dancers.
A stranger calls. He claims he's dropped from space.

You sit in a leopard-spot leotard,
playing the piano with one toe.
You want the big number. The stranger stays,
ten zeros on his silver identity card.

NEW LANDSCAPE

It could be singular, your visit there,
arrival through a dream that you've sustained
awake, no interruptions in the flow,
just a vague filmic pressure which starts to slow
and isolate a tabula rasa
impression that the new landscape
is filling in for you. The thin blue air
that flickered with red fish shapes form Paul Klee,
clears to a green transparency.
A mesa is defined in the foreground,
a single columned white house built on its summit
invites enquiry. Perhaps you've come home
to appropriate an exclusive space?
Windows are open on four different skies,
four different colours: yellow, black, blue, red.
Inside a girl lies dreaming on a bed,
one gartered white leg and one black.
She shuts her eyes and leaves you to explore
each aquariumed floor. Gold fish show through.
Mirrors create infinity,
and when at last you pass through the interior
and open a door to the patio,
it is to find you're on the edge of space.
Glass buildings are going up in the sky,
but they're unreachable. You go inside
and as you move a glass wall follows you
and builds to an unbreaking wave.
You turn round and the house has disappeared
on its mesa. A glass cliff-face
divides you from a sea that's fast and blue.

THE WAY OUT

We left because our narrative would claim
the cities we had dreamt and knew were there
to be discovered. Ruby In The Dust,
Pink Mirage, Upper Grasslands – they were names
leaked to us by underground radio,
parallel stations. We'd hit on their air
by spontaneous tuning and grown obsessed
stayed up each night, news of another world
in our own language bending how we thought
to new considerations. We were hooked.

We drove out of the fall; a copper glare
in red maples – a girl beside the road
waving to us: yellow and green
filling stations punctuating the way,
everything recognized until a jump
in the sequence informed us we were through
to a parallel country. The same day,
a silver convertible striped with blue,
ahead of us, our radio broadcast
talking of gynaecology, women
who'd been up in orbit, a carnival
at Ruby In The Dust, an invasion
we couldn't catch . . . So it was really true,
we'd exchanged one reality
for another – a blue sky overhead,
a fixed aircraft, preliminaries snatched
before we reached the city, found no one,
and lifted our arms to the setting sun.

A WARNING

The cloud was early on us, a black square
that came and went, a tarpaulin
stretched tight across the horizon
bringing the shadow down, the periodic threat
of change to our small lives, the race sterile,
our species hoping to inseminate
by thought forms, sex directed by a ray,
the child born from the fantasy:
blue men, green women, mauve hermaphrodites,
gold mutants, and their chemistry
evolving a polysexual species.

We left our offices, our homes, and went
to stand under the cloud. Indoors we felt
trapped inside a black ink bottle
and suffocating in the dark.
It seemed better in the open, the park
with its wide oval lawn, our cars ready
to take us to coastal limitations.
Mostly we feared the cloud would stay
and we'd get wide of it to blue edges
and see its localized concentration
as something personal : a cloud man issue.
This time we came down to the red alert
and found orderly places in the crowd
and looked upwards and saw a red and blue
concentric eye in the opacity,
a thin ray leaking down, touching no one,
forming a spotlit circle on the grass,
our buildings lit up, exposed, and the first
breaking for their cars to begin the flight.

THE CHEMICAL LIFE

The implant receptor feeds on the drug;
he tells her that as her fellatio
works him to a tulip's pink head,
still compact, tight; he's an experiment
for robot research. Outside the window
people are gathered on rooftops,
looking again for the UFO patrol,
the twenty red and silver tops which slowed
above the city, waited and came low
over the packed arena; a singer
tongue-teasing the microphone, while guitars
raked feedback through stratocasters.
And now the people await a return
visit from the aliens; they feel alone,
forgotten on one of the tiny stars.

Jane's tongue has a snake-like facility.
She coaxes him and makes him wait.
'In two years, I'll be someone else,' he says,
'dependent on a pharmaceutical
and without an earth-memory.
The space invaders will have taken me
to a parallel world that is so near
it lives inside the chemical.' Their son
listens outside the door in his space-suit.
Jane will not stop now and his triggering
is focused to release a sun
inside his head that's luminous, a bright
planet that burns out like a meteor.

WAITING

Creatures of stress, we take our time on trust.
We can't like the lizard drop our tail in
                                    the dust,
and live regeneratively sunning on a stone,
grass-green, pulsing. A quick emerald flash . . .
We're charred and on a thinning line,
uncertain as we've always been
of going on or what the future means
except we're always getting there.
And are it.

Possible visuals come to mind.
The waiting. Long haired men out on the coast
living in communities, their women
with mauve and scarlet hair. Waiting.
A broken clock sits on the sand.
The sun lifts too close and dangerously.
They do not understand.
Jets keep coming in low over the land,

then silence, more waiting.
Something may happen. Not an end.
I think they're swimming in the rising sea.

ANGULAR

THREE DECADES OF JAGGER

And that's too little for uncompromise,
raising a whiphand to conformity;
the skinny, unkempt schoolboy in hipsters,
mean with maracas, pulling a surprise

on the establishment's dead machismo,
daring to make a fashion of long hair,
high-heeled boots, pouting so the negroid lips
made the wide ovoid of fellatio

around a phallic microphone. And live,
so dynamized, an electric dervish
slowing to a falsetto blues; few thought
your hyped-up extroversion would survive

more than a year or two; but you had air,
that unnamed particle which once released
is self-expansive, power that blows through walls,
its hard pressure pinpointed in your stare

that goes on holding crowds in abeyance;
now it is mega-stadiums, hard rock,
and you're still energized, youthful, a slap
to the disclaimers who you will outdance

a lifetime. You're from Egon Schiele's art,
one hand on the hip, a contortionist's
agility – prototypal rebel,
we think no love-arrow could pierce your heart

because you're everyone's; and what you've made
from public confrontation is a role
that liberates and grows to a statement
about ourselves; how we are less afraid

to be the individual. Look, you say,
the age grows with us: the music is tight
and graduates, the vocals pitched up high.
The town is closed because you're on today.

FOR MARC ALMOND

The lyric bounces from the street
into our hands as a red ball.
My poetry and your invasive voice
find somewhere a congruity,

the fifth side to a square; a catch
in regulated breath; the word
that flies off as a frightened bird
to live with others. You launch it through notes,

I keep it on the page. It's death
as a symbolic variant
provides the tension to create.
When words are there I walk clean through a wall.

Dejected hubris. It's a blue-blue note
I hear from a window in your street.
You might be composing an elegy
for pink culture, piano-smudging a beat

to have the blue tone lift. It rains outside.
I walk to meet the day as an idea
about the poem I'm writing.
Orange panopticons are like a sun

in the fruit market. It's a testing thing
this writing on one's nerves. Later I'll try
your Melancholy Rose as a prelude
to a new mood that settles at evening.

THE POETRY WORLD

So little light ever reaches that grey
collective mediocrity a wolf
can terrorize. They're mostly seen in groups,
misshapen, badly dressed, incestuous,
exponents of the ordinary,
opponents of the visionary;
journalists, academics, none would risk
the cutting-edge, the standing out alone

to make of life and poetry one art.
I don't find there an eye which sees beauty
in anything; the whiplash tornado
of the imagination's power to hunt
like a cheetah's accelerative drive –
a kicked-up dust-storm – doesn't register
in this luded out Earls Court mortuary.
Stone eyes, stone heart, stone feet;
the one rule's self-advancement: play it right
and he might publish me.
Their safety-net is Larkin's provincial
de-sexualized climacteric; the flat
sensibility bred by a library.

Imagination's better on the street,
picking up vibrancy or anywhere
the light transforms experience
into discovery. The never seen before
realized through a minted imagery.
A forest leading to a desert to the sea.
I keep away from the huddle. Tonight
I'll lose myself in something that has beat.

PINK CULTURE

And is it better for the out. I see
diminished tension, more transparency

in what was always there, but different.
And yes, Rimbaud would have made an event

of marching; defiant, keyed with outrage,
spiky hair, mobbing for the centre-stage,

then turning his back, bored with everything,
most likely unravelling a red string

to play with an imaginary kitten.
What seems instructive, best, is a mauve pen

drawing another species with the line
of Cocteau or Matisse; the androgyne

re-invented, taking something from all
and owing nothing; it's an integral

solution under no banner; I see
the mutants swarm out of the century

into the future. Is it Jupiter
or Mars they gravitate to in answer

to expendable factions? The pink has made
it possible; living true, unafraid

of identity – a link to the race
now falling earthwards, tilting a new face.

ROCK AND POETRY

One feeds the other. It's the subversive
I value – speed injected into words,
the volatile flash lifting syllables
into a rain forest of coloured birds,

a storm of scarlet, green and gold.
Poetry needs street-cred, an energy
vital to youth; two standing out the rain
in Greek Street, reading their own memory

of now and what it means to be alive
in someone else's words. *He* got it right,
rain moving in out of a blue cloud ridge
makes brilliant statements about the light,

accents the April day and tinctures it
like the black corolla inside a flower.
And there's another way to make it live;
her Walkman starts to crackle with the power

of menacing feedback: a voice cuts in
that's separated by the mix; it too
speaks of an up day through a minimal
novella; a red car pursues a blue,

the girl smiling at the boy at the lights,
then slipping away into dense traffic
is lost for ever, an elusive blonde
he thinks of in his solitary attic,

and the guitars chase her all over town . . .
It's a dynamic: rock and poetry
meeting in individual ways
to make sense of our age, of you and me

welcoming each liberative gesture
that gets us nearer cutting the ribbon
on impositions, living to the full
and celebrating how that freedom's won.

MODERN MYTHS

They're in the making if we turn around
to snap the picture; but the light's too fast,
the image disperses across the speed
of living. Vision filters into sound,

a dissonance that's with us all the way;
the singer snaked up to a microphone,
reality a film-set flickering
into impermanence. And will you stay?

not you beside me with your purple hair,
but anyone who's made a mark; are we
too many or too few names on a wall
that's always breaking down and hardly there

for the inclusion of our desperate
enforcement that we were around a year
or two, confused by changes? You and I
sit drinking on a pavement, and it's late

in time. We no longer have Picasso
to alter how we see and what we see
and make of it a culture. The film-reel
spins crazily. You make a lipstick bow

and pout it into shape; and day by day
what's permanent remains half-realized,
and it may lie partly in how we look
as much as anything, for that's a way

of art purposeful to the face, the street,
to individual expression, and you
put on a leather cap to match your boots,
uncertain who in tonight's myth you'll meet.

MODERN LOVE

Her sister's postered room; freebies, fanzines,
the singer's nympholeptic lips,
red-hot, faking it for the video:
T.T. a snake in leather as she slips

into Private Dancer, a husky blues
voice tuned to funk. An alien leans
against a violet wall – an arts school doll,
robotic, sprayed silver. The young girl's jeans

are crisscross slashed, tagged with logos,
so contoured she bends from the waist
and lowers herself to her knees
for lack of give. Thumbtacks and paste,

an airbrush and her make-up bag
spill on her counterpane – a red love-heart
pierced by a cupid's arrow: *I'm too hot.*
He sits in the other room, acts his part

as moody and misunderstood,
his cactus resin gel makes him the man
the record and film scouts have missed.
His double is an abreactive fan.

He leans back from the soundless screen.
A New-York facade: anodized
aluminium – the cops have just pulled up
for narco-cartels they've surprised

in Lexington. They each do their own thing.
Language replaced by visuals; and in bed
a poster has glossy black thigh-high boots
walking on air above her head.

GRAFFITI ARTIST

The red graffiti sprayed across a wall
in sanskrit ciphers is my clue today
to something obvious that's drifted wide
of meaning. Written up to stay,
the air-brush calligraphist's left a skull
dead centre to his cryptic diagram;
and at the street corner a red arrow
points upwards to the sky. He left that way,
or so I like to think or disappeared
into the night with his fragmented text
punctuating his journey through alleys,
one startling visual leading to the next
and non-sequential: each a found poem

that lives like segments of a chopped up snake.
What is his language? It's intentional
and recognizably linked to our own;
a sort of latter day prophetic script
that works like a director's speeded take,
jolting the senses to a colour flash,
a violent red, green or fluorescent pink.
I could follow his trail, pick through the trash
for his individual cut-ups and read
a future in his day-glo dialect,
and perhaps in time complete the story
he's left open-ended.

                              Imagine it,
meeting him in the process of his art,
a parking lot at 2 a.m.: concealed,

not wishing to intrude, watching his hand
engaged in a vocabulary, his line
hurried, embellished: a cap on his head,
and on his denim back, a purple heart.

AT THE MIXER

From Passaic to Padua
the man negotiates prospective art,
it's the idea he sells, air-brush frescos
in yellow, scarlet and ultramarine.
Not chaos, but its configuration,
not Rothko, but a different resonance,
a house painted by rooms, a scarlet heart
in the bedroom, a black cross sprayed across
a whitewashed room in which to die,
a blue room, red room, his academy
move in a week and feel the way,
even a psycho can respond
to colour vibration and help himself
blowing red aerosols across a wall
instead of killing. The man has mystique,
stays in a white hotel above the bay
and won't give interviews. His method's personal.
It finds the colour tints of an aura,
a rhythm in the nerves – he has the call
and uses it in exchange for money.
He leaves a bedroom washed out black and blue
with elementary white clouds, when serene,
but most often it's the bathroom
he chooses, white on white a latent moon
has risen in his mind, an abstract place,
but sometimes there's a thin red line of blood
that enigmatically he calls the clue.

A WALK IN THE BLACK FOREST

The children left too early. Years ago
they migrated to a hidden country,
a scattering that left no individual name,
only the memory of light dispersed

before a violent storm. We have survived
their going, and you point me to a tree
on which initials survive in the grain.
Déjà vu makes our looking seem rehearsed:

were we part of the hurried exodus,
and have we taken on what we disclaimed,
the adventure of change and age? Cities
have indexed us with stress, an inventory

of fragmented days, the glass thrown up high
because the bottle's empty. They are gone,
the ones who lived in tree houses, apart,
trusting a ladder to reach for the sky

and not come down. Cloud shadows map the ground;
we think of the future as screened like deer
cautiously listening in a quiet place.
The events will bolt out of deep cover.

We want to know what happened; why they left
and if they're gathered somewhere in a space
that's still unclaimed; children living to know
the secret in just being, not grown old

because that is a conscious act, a way
we seem to want to inherit, not lose.
We'll find them one day in a black forest,
a gold stag at their feet. Perhaps they'll stay.

UNDERGROUND

We meet inside the night. You show me how
a red and mauve Javanese mask tattoo
is kited from an articulate vine
straggling your shoulder. We are just below

the line of visibility; a wall
divides us from the others. There's a bar
gives on to the river, and green neon
chimes on the black. We're waiting for a call

which is directional. I seem to hear
myself listening in silence since childhood
for a nocturnal voice, a lost ship's horn.
A silver deathshead hangs from your left ear.

And living out of line's intentional;
it's easier to build purpose that way,
meet up with a fraternity. The light
that hits my words is unconditional,

it shares with us a means to make it clear
that there is power in minorities,
a strength in standing out, picking up pace
by being less cluttered. We're very near

a death to the old orders. What is that? –
a stone lion rinsed clean by white lightning,
or someone so solitary they're made new?
We're startled by the snake-thrust of a cat

tailing a tin can as it makes the quay.
And there are others now, come out the dark.
They sit around and talk. The night is young,
and the earth old with misidentity.

NEW WAVE

The storm's delayed. A bottle of mauve ink
thrown at a white wall, the jagged asterisk
abruptly shattering, the radial stain
darkening, allows no time for the link

to form; it happened and the centre broke
without warning like the impacted glass
in Magritte's window: how did it occur,
from the inside or out? No one awoke

until they dreamt the fracture. What's around
is too immediate for most. The things
I do in private in a darkened room,
or the subversive, undercutting sound

of a fast band in black shades takes me to
extremities, the dangerous outer rim
where everything is very clear. I find
exhilaration coming at the new

from an oblique strategy. A leopard
will stalk by scent, describing a circle
before it breaks cover and where it hits
forces a hurricane. In the back yard

two kids with a ghetto-blaster attack
a cultural complacency. They jerk
out a mime-dance to dissonance; one wears
a deathshead logo on his leather back;

both have scuffed jeans. They're pointing to a space
that's still unoccupied by art; the risk
is there to be explored. They cut the track,
high-kick and disappear without a trace.

GEORGE

for Alan

Generous man, exuberant with life,
your big hands carrying Jamaican warmth,
you come back busy in my memory
as my eye turns on colours at this stall,
pineapple, mango, avocado, peach,
exotic fruits that I associate with you
by temperament. We knew your buoyancy,
your spontaneity, and how you lived
for simple things, the pulsing reggae beat
or pop that sounded from your room.
A tear snakes right across my memory,
smelling these fruits and knowing you won't taste
their scent again. That last time in the hall
with Alan, how could I know it for that,
a valediction: you on a spiral
of such agonizingly speeded-up decline,
there wasn't time to ever talk again,
you living out your last weeks, unconscious;
no word could get through. Now a beady rain

delays me at this street market. I think
of your obsessive array of colognes
and how I read their names, and of the clothes
you loved, stylish, flamboyant as the dahlias
you cultivated: red, yellow and white,
spiky crowns, little sea-anemones.
Displaced in London, you carried the sun
inside you, waiting only to return
to islands. And your gift was love;

the one that's missed by he who shared your life
and waits to know if you're alright. You are.
We sense that. Generosity translates
into the spirit. Now the rain gives off.
The glaze around me lights up like a star.

TALKING BACK TO THE POEM

We form a unity and where we split
the flaw is evident. My deference
goes half the way; I make the pieces fit

and look for shock; that staggering deep pink
of cherry blossom lifting windy skirts
has caught us both. A mood-switch; when I drink

or take my senses to extremes, I try
to do it my style, gain the ascendant;
see if you follow when I start to fly

with loud music, colours mixed to suggest
Matisse's palette after LSD.
My wild storm puts both of us to the test;

a black girl in a gold g-string will hook
her legs over my shoulders. It is time
to stimulate the poem and I look

for whatever will excite, run outside
into the rain after sex for a blue
that's showing through, a blue out of the tide

known at Arcachon; and you haven't gone,
despite my distractions, but send me back
to re-evaluate what I have done.

It's a joint effort, and where we combine
the power's lethal; serpents in the cracks
are my invention and their gold scales shine.

DRINKING DOWN UNDER

It blows one back, but there's lucidity
in this method, positive over-reach
to have and do; hallucinated, free

to walk the world's roof without scaffolding,
fired by tequila's yellow sun or high
on a red Bordeaux, almost anything

we know is right for us: delayed or quick
to hit the nerves. It is a ritual,
an implosive instigator; my kick

is feeling it take off – the vertigo
of seeing things alter shape. The mad flash
that turns a flower to a Chagall window.

Pollock ran at his surface, naked, lit
by bourbon, Bacon came at distortion
shot through with liquor; all the odd planes fit

into the anamorph. Lowry, Hart Crane,
so many poets binged, anaesthetized
against reality, worked on their pain

by translating it into wild vision.
I find my level; it's optimistic,
not schizoid, morose, but a fast action

lift off into another dimension,
so many hours up, then a levelling out.
I live for that: the smashing of caution.

THE LOST IDEAL

It shines no less intensely for its loss,
poetry as an absolute, a way
to realization under blue April skies.
The gift gives back where light lives in the hand.

I find it anywhere I look around,
it's written into faces, cut in trees.
I make it out on the white page
before the pen responds with ink.

It is a living continuity
this contact made despite disparagement.
This little shop where I buy stationery
is sometimes luminous with poetry.

And they are everywhere its enemies –
dead-fingered editors, the media's
swallowing on ephemera:
corruption as it speaks through lies.

The light is interested in speaking through
its voices. They are overheard
sometimes, the poem seen like a crystal
suspended in the hurried shower.

Mostly one stays alone and gives to all
what must be found. It's years later
the poem reports back to the poet.
'I came to you one spring, and now it's fall . . .'

UPPER RED

And where the debris littered, he'd retrieved
the pilot's black box, combed the mountain grass
for atomized disjecta, cut his hand
on a fine hail of sharded glass
and quit the place, zipping his white sportscar

towards a stone retreat, with pinkish snow
still forming napkins on the upper slopes
and in the distance a helicopter
circling to target the jigsaw below,
blown across needles when the fuel lit up

and seemed to rip a fracture in the sky.
And he was always on that frequency
of intersecting with catastrophe,
a speed-age freak – he lived up in the air,
ledged between pines, a high altitude lodge

with a blue glass observatory
and swarms of red fish screened around the walls
flickering into view like meteors.
It was his hide-out. Curiosity
and mood mutations had him gravitate

towards the unhinging, then he'd be gone
back to his isolation, lost for weeks
in a speculative metaphysics,
turning his question round on a pinpoint,
deliberating like someone who seeks

absolute clarity in a heat-flash,
a crystal forming from a smashed windshield,
vision at that point where the mind blacks out;
and checks the road, the black box in his lap,
his mind racing to restructure the crash.

THE ODD IN POETRY

The black knot in the apple I'm inside.
The tang is bitter, but I'm this far now
to know the headiness. If I should hide

from the tenting shadow, I'd lose the way
to moments when the light dazzles, transforms
incidents of an ordinary day.

Often I worry about poverty –
the face-down side of words. They take me where
my health's at risk, but I have learnt to see

the interior of things, quiet like a deer
reading the wind for scent. Sometimes I stray
into a landscape of voluntary fear –

that's *me*, and there's my double looking down
from zigzag fire-stairs; but he cannot speak.
I do not think I know this part of town.

And there's no compromise. I can't turn back,
the momentum accelerates, in luck
or out, I know the markings on my track,

the human breakage. Look what I have done,
severed every security, burnt out
myself and others for the poems won

by risk, by sacrifice. And celebrate
the beauty given in particulars;
the first star each evening, for which I wait.

GOTH POP

The blond one scratches a guitar solo,
a needling antipathy to the crowd
packing the stage; his mean virtuoso

phased out by bass and the singer's return
under the pooled spotlights. Red, blue and green.
They're laid back. Only the encore will burn.

New songs are aired tonight. They're hermetic,
minimally arranged; the dark squeezed out
from a grey lemon. Shrill feedback, static.

The band play on the edge; a lyric flash
has purple thunder break on the highway.
A red car activates a head on crash.

The initiates lean towards each word.
In fun wigs and jagged leather, they're a cult.
They live by intimation, lines half-heard,

a stuttered eloquence, drawled monotone.
They're nearing the penultimate death-push.
The singer's backed up by a gel-haired clone.

Crouched low, a cortege behind dry-ice screens,
the song drags to an improvised climax.
Drugs are the problem in her hung up teens.

They end abruptly; the song's slashed in two;
and leave the crowd with the expectancy
of the killed number and of course they're through.

SPOOK

I codify your number, and the tone
assures me you're not there: an empty room?
I hang up on myself. I am alone,

you needn't be. All over the city,
nervous impulses are feeding the wires;
the hidden illusionist says he's *me*,

and you form features round the voice. An age,
a possible face, eyes, sensuous lips.
You're in the dark, and I'm standing offstage;

the process works both ways. We call it trust.
And what of spooking, audial poltergeists?
That sort say they need it, and so they must.

I try again to call you up, locate
you in your thoughts. You might be undressing,
reading a book. I don't think it's too late.

I mustn't let the thing grow obsessive,
a finger-marksman tuning in all night.
We all need privacy in which to live

outside of reach. The house lights on around
my darkened room, tell me that it is night.
In the receiver there's a voice I've found:

who are you? Why are you silent again?
What do you want? And then the line goes dead.
My ear fills with the sudden brief of rain.

THE ESTABLISHMENT

They inhabit another continent,
all sheep, no wolves, a huddled mediocrity
that looks to the collective to shelter
dead impulses. All birds on that island
have stone wings and can never lift and know the sky's
blue spaces or the generosity
that lives in the creative. They are flat
like their grey buildings; equally as flawed
as stucco fissures mapped on a highrise.
Their dead books shuttle to the fire
of a crematorium's oven.
Their fraudulent public faces don't see
beauty or how originality
animates the image to poetry.

I sit, back to the wall in a basement.
I write, and five purple tulips instruct
me love and the word are evident;
I, and my life as an outsider, free.

SKY HIGH

The logo on his T-shirt reads Sky High,
a blue rectangle inserted on red,

a yellow rocket on its launching-pad.
The sea keeps bringing pieces of the sky

ashore, blue fractured planes, alto-cirrus.
His topless girlfriend wears a leather tie

and reads Interzone; a Ballard story
set in the 22nd century . . .

His Walkman puts him in touch with the age,
street language, minimal semiotics,

they want the future, but immediacy
is all they have, the landscape dead, the day

pushed forward on their active frequency
by two thousand years. He is high on crack

and sees the lighthouse as a white cactus
issuing from an aquatic desert.

They never speak; they have it all on trust,
their inter-alienation; and a jet

crashes through the blue windowpane of space.
His logo reads true; he is flying high

in his deserted place. She holds his hand:
she might be reaching for him from the sky.

ARSONIST

Derelict. He slept in basements,
cocooned in paper; his black suit
concertinaed, his face bricky, raw,
hedgehogged with silver stubble.

Dust was his irritant, caked hands
he longed to cool in the river
he'd fly-fished in childhood
feeling his mauve fly shiver

the eddies. If it was a smell, a light
communicated to him as a source
of estrangement, it was the rage
repressed as fire that made it worse.

He'd got to know interiors,
night watchmen, and the image of a fox
bolting from the first blaze he'd lit
in furze, remained indelibly russet.

The pressure building in dry heat,
he knew it had to be out, something burn
other than his disordered nerves.
He hallucinated flames at his feet

and shrank from policemen, passersby.
That day he kept in a warehouse,
knowing he'd do it, there was gasoline
and turpentine left by painters,

rats and a dead one jewelled by flies.
The rear gave on to an apartment block.
He came out at night hypnotized
by his inner vision; the shock

would jolt him back into reality,
watching among the crowds the roaring crack
of flames fissure a building, turning round,
calm, with the fire reflected on his back.

THINGS WE DO

Pink sunlight lays an evenly diffused
rhomboid on the studio floor. Two men
sit beneath heart-shaped silver balloons
discussing how they connect with the world,

their access to current, the power-switch
that's always out of reach. The mint julep
in tall glasses remains untouched.
The fashion model returns to retrieve

a leather jacket and a felt-tip pen.
She is distracted until touch confirms
the question of her memory.
She puts on shades. The light spots on her knees;

her mind anticipates a luncheon date,
a kiss that tastes of strawberry
between appointments. The taxi is late.
The two men talk of video,

and how to live invisibly,
despatching pre-recorded films
to colleagues, friends, establishing a cult
of presence through absence, using that blank

to make oblique raids on experience.
One's dressed in cashmere, the other in jeans;
they are a partnership and only speak
of new artificial intelligence.

The one in jeans prepares to photograph
another fashion sequence, so they split,
each coming at the real from a tangent:
the model makes the tight skirt fit.

OUTSIDERS

The tidal increase or its out
brought me to edges; it was the blue sill
beyond which I couldn't advance,
a back-off level, I returned

to a child's frustrated biography,
one foot cut on the hewn sea-steps,
trailing little mulberry blotches of blood.
My mind was with the unpredictables,

the ones who come at things from the outside
and threaten with their unrestrained
destabilizing art. A dust-storm raised
between the covers of a book.

Impatience. I read Michaux's *Ecuador*,
the cosmonauts of inner space.
Life was like squeezing an orange
into a rose. A reckless energy

had me imagine the out-there,
a world I had prepared to take by storm.
The black bull in our farmer's field
nursed the same frustration. A mad orbit

that swung out to the stars.
I nurtured my gift with the odd,
the questionable to the law;
each poem was a loaded gun,

and still I quiver at the sights,
aiming always for an oblique target
with an outsider's range to make my hit
ring true and disappear.

LEARNING IT YOUNG

It is something privileged: living fast
without the cluttered drag of age,
anticipation in the air,
like waiting for the band to come on stage

wired to a lethal circuitry.
Everything may still happen. Look, her mouth
is open to catch the hailstone's
fast scintilla, and the flurry's like youth,

jolted, buoyant and unpredictable,
born of the moment, running where
the impulse directs. He has gelled,
and she combed-out, henna-red hair.

What's in, what's out; the image shares
a street-face, then goes to the wall.
Deletions are spontaneous,
'I didn't write,' he says, 'I'd rather call

to say it's over. Someone new.'
Always a first dawn, redder, promising
travel, a convertible to Toulouse,
wine on the road, no ties, and existing

to kick the fire out of dead ash,
to hear the compacted cork detonate,
burning to meet the sudden rush
of frenzy at a surprise date,

not slowing down, running from youth to death
with no intermediary years.
There on the street-corner they've lit a fire,
hoping a backward ethos disappears.

LETTERS

A surf of rectangles. I'm always late
to prune the jumble, the panopticons
of a disordered spate;
a cataract that's left to spill.

Sometimes they're like square snow-prints on table
and floor, and variegated, black and pink
or red and blue, a mosaic
frescoed with stamps, black-ink

medallions. The ones I recognize,
the ones I don't and open cautiously
for the wasp or the butterfly
unfolding from the page.

Fifteen a day. A global avalanche;
a dependably reassuring fall.
They crackle in my hands, wallets, sachets,
a paper artichoke I unpetal

to reach the heart.
And each so individual
in ways that letters admit more than speech,
are orchestrated by mood and personal

obsessions, leitmotivs, and if we met
we'd find each other different,
shrugging those issues, making light
of what goes deep; the stone in the dark core.

I fish the pile and forget none;
it's like the childhood game in which
I didn't look and with a magnet on a string
retrieved topheavy cardboard carp

from an aquarium. I test the feel.
We're lifelines to each other; paper birds
launched on impossible trajectories.
We leave our flight-runs; little scores of words . . .

RETRIEVALS

The wind scuffs sand into a gold dust cloud,
a furious equinoctial finale
to a long summer; an open sea-door,
white chair and table on a balcony

pointing to a curved beach, a marina,
and somewhere, hazed out, the opposite coast –
a mauve premonition of Normandy,
its surf-line clear for intervals, then lost

as a half-realized configuration.
Summer's a mirror held to youth? its days
are plotted like a ship's course on a chart;
blue intervals mirrored by bluer bays.

Each year we think it's there extensibly,
the light is movement and we go with it
towards an imagined ideal that life
is always ours; the leonine sunset

succeeded by a pea-green dawn, the ease
of slipping into the new day, ostensibly
defined by it . . . And when the fissure shows,
white caps beating time to a faster sea,

so people disappear, pronounce an end
to slacker limpid hours, and smoke-screened by
the lifting sand, go as a procession . . .
We thought we'd outlive death, not live to die . . .

STOOD UP

She hardly notices how sunlight frames
a climbing red rose spiralling
the house wall opposite.
She shifts the balance on her heels, her mood

of anticipation losing
to anger, bitterness, a fear
that something's happened which she can't control.

An ambulance siren? – the inflexion
of his last spoken word two hours ago,
the urgency of one, the hesitance
of the other, and both are wrong,
too fast, too slow.

She checks her watch; the time and place
co-ordinated for safety.
She knows about his wife, the inner scars

that leak through, and after love, confession.
She audio-hallucinates his voice,
breathtaking arrival. The netted gold
has shifted from the wall.
                                        She starts to go,
and keeps on walking, disconsolate, cold.

TOAD

The one I rescued from a cat: so small
it seemed a nimble brooch cupped in my hands,
a coolness imparted to warmth,
immobile, unprotesting, flippery,
I carried it back from that lit alley
one hot night in July, dry, thundery,
the air stubbornly ungiving, a match
and the heath would crackle, jump with red flame.

You followed as I nursed our red-eyed captive,
skin mottled like army dungarees,
a yellow pebbling on the sage-green skin
with buffs and earth-browns pigmented
by way of camouflage. How could it know
my intentions, this rapid conveyance;
a warm pulse thudding at its cool?

We placed it undercover
in a dark corner; and fat spots of rain
arrived in answer to a sympathy
coextensible between us and it,
the two month drought terminated, the shower
torrential, steamy, bubbling into cracks.
We came alive after the walled heat,

and thought of our domestic talisman,
little chthonic household god,
provident with blessings, and this perhaps
the first of many prompted felicities?
We flung the windows wide on the night rain,

its silver sluicing through the dense lime trees.

WINTER POEM

You come into my life again, black ink
stitching your narrative across the page.
We can't be as we were I've said,
the loop's twisted to opposing spirals,
yet still you traffic fiction for a life
we've severed, tail and head
despatched as parts thrown in a field.
A butchered snake that can't reintegrate.
You've made your boots out of its chequered skin.

Winter finds you in a new part
of the forest. Right out of town.
You need the ice to cool your heart,
you say; the deer to console with black eyes
that seem lifted from wells. The other you
resents the self-imposed exile.
Your crazier, self-destructive short fuse
still needs to burn and blow. You're like a stoat
that puts its teeth in its own throat
for lack of prey.
                              Your Northern winter's hard,
but brilliant in its clarity.
I imagine you as the solitary
walker in blue woods, and each change of mood
contradicting what you will write
to me at nightfall, staring out lonely
at the snow-dazzle, the increasing white.

OCTOPUS

Invertebrate chimera,
flexing an octet of snakes
with their rubber suction-pads,
a bald pink sponge compacted
into a hole and watching.

Its shape belongs to the hypnagogic
nebulae that precede sleep.
Images that surface to go deep
again and crop up intermittently
like the octopus, drill-hole eyes and bony mouth.
As a child I saw one turned inside out,
a caution shown by fishermen
to prevent the blinding inkcap's black emission.
Its blue-black tear-gas when pursued.

Gelatinous,
a dead octopus
is like a diseased internal organ,
not to be seen, not to be touched,
but is cut into strips for bait
and trailed. It's gorgonic, tentacular,

an imitative Medusa
hidden under wrack at low tide
in shallow gulleys. It's meditative
and copes from concealment.

Draw it out and it's honest to its type.
A breathing muscle, weaponry
adapted to its needs, an unevolved

creation – prototype,
holding on to its method to the end –

its primal, scent-instructed continuity.

AUBRETIA

The shock of mauve aubretia; how it's there
like us and not knowing why, surprising
by its intensity beneath a pink

cherry blossom. I'm arrested
by its violet graciousness – how it links
to a deeper level in me
a childhood reality

that mauve flower shocking the length of a wall
concealing a farm, meaning spring
was intrusive again with showers,
inseparable from the illusory
belief we come back like the leaf
uncurling from the alder. Greener-green.

That we don't live contemporaneous
with things is what that flower imparts today,
no less livid for its bright rain-washed mauves,
and oddly like a Russian
symbolist poem,
ephemeral, pointing the way
to death – our own personal revolution.

YACHT HOTEL
for Jon Godfrey

Our meetings on a needle-point,
there's never time to formulate
our satelliting impromptu
salvos, I'm here a week and gone
although it cuts me to the bone . . .

Everything changes to the eye,
my island home accelerates
the greed by which it dominates
the tax-dominions. The lighthouse
we look out at plays cat and mouse

with the night-waters; now it's dead,
the daylight streams with urgent cars;
they'll get there but not to the stars . . .
We sit and drink. My poetry,
your photographs, mean nothing here,

expendables on the index
by which man lives: committed art
like gold-dust on a granite heart;
it's the coastline we hold to, blue
and pine-green bays pacing a view

across the Gulf of St Malo,
the light's painterly quality
mirrored by a kingfisher sea.
Pure symmetry, the light expands
to a bridge meeting the white sands

on the French side. Here we're in town;
a harbour prospect, and above
the casino's glass cupola
turns diamond and then luminous
beneath the shower. A banker's crown.

Tomorrow I fly out. Our words
leave the future open-ended.
Time changes us faster than we
can check, tired creatures hurrying
to meet with the new century.

GRAPE HYACINTHS

And come again
obedient to the recurring cycle,
no omissions, the hyacinth-scented

blue-lavender lobes pointing to a cone,
an assertion they are and individually
their own identity upon this earth.
If they had memory

they'd tell of dark beginnings, consciousness
taking colour from the light-waves,
the schema that impregnated the earth,

the dream-flash seeding a reality.
Little blue curly phallic-tip
on so green a polished stem
in numbers for assurance that the code
is never written out generically,

your return reinvokes the trust
we've lost in things remaining as they are:
flower, mineral, water, star.

TILT

We lie contoured in grass beneath squat oaks;
the valley rings beneath us with its stream;
the light is hay-blond, and the shadows run
like black fire distributed by the wind.

An ordinary day? Yet there's a tilt,
as though a glass inclined and stayed that way;
its contents suspended above the earth.
I feel displaced, and now a frenzied jay

tears at the silence. Other couples sit,
lost in the high grass, or two lovers thresh
a jade swimming-pool in the raffish bank.
The heat settles down and we're part of it;

light in its free-fall defining detail,
things which we name and which don't really mean
unless we charge the word with resonance.
The world is abstract becoming concrete.

A leather couple, each with purple hair,
have brought their child, and it acknowledges
their radio as apotheosis.
They hit the world obliquely, off-beat, wild;

we catch their drift of music. Air and air.
The hour is gold and we lack connections
to make it real, it's disappearing past
studied frontiers that might have had it last.

And now a pink kite lifts above the trees,
fish-hesitant, swimming in the blue air.
We watch it fluctuate. Longevity
is yours; an oak leaf flighted in your hair.

STARS WAITING ON MOUNTAINS

And sometimes, latterly, they understand
the messages transmitted on cassette
and sent them in black envelopes.
Nearer, their father writes about the farm,
the ruined seasons and how a white horse
swam right across the mountain lake
and came to his front door and stayed.
That was 100 years ago. His snaps
illustrate how he's changed, and one autoportrait
presents a double. The child that he was
peers through a mop-haired fringe
over a bony left shoulder.
One day, the child will say to him, follow,
and they will mount the horse and swim all day
and night to complete the journey.
And he will know the place, sit on a gold boulder,
leave the child fish for salmon with the bears.
The distance hardly matters.

Sometime they write their father. 'We're not far,
but since the audios arrived we seem
detached, estranged. Last night the snow was mauve,
the couple came from a near star
and helped us decipher their messages.
We may go with them when we are informed;
and your white horse would have turned purple here
beneath the flurry.
                              Jill's gone in her car
towards our highest peak. I'm left behind,
impatient to have news, but anyhow
what we're both doing must seem very clear.'

RAWHIDE

Swathe of the meadow beard and cows lie down.
Indolent bulks brought to their knees,
curded mouths, rubbery nostrils, brown eyes
that crawl with spotting flies –
globe-trotters on gelatinous
convexities. The cows rhythmically swish

their stringy tails in time
to irritation.
These Jerseys are red, small statured like deer,
and lie like stranded hulks.
Grey dandelion helmets wobble fluffily
and rake the air. Cows seem to come so far

in looking out from who they are
to where their vision goes. If it stops flat
at the immediate, seeing's a wall
run up against another wall.
Some have rolled over clean on to their flanks

and the flies stick; vibrating jewelled pustules.
Give a cow wings and its crash course
would be in the same meadow.
They're unshiftable from the here and now

and purposeful mashing viridian cud.
I fire metaphors at their hide
or try to dimensionalize a way in.
They are resilient. They're stepping stones
to thought across a green hay flood.

FORGET-ME-NOT

Bringing the sky down to the earth

a blue density, little yellow-eyed
azure myosotis, so true
a blue, each stem a star-cluster,
blizzarding earthy nebulae
risen from a component green.

I find you out by streams or grown up wild
in this garden. You meet the blue
in me as once De Nerval found
the visionary you in a dark night street.
A blue hallucinated star.

We share no consciousness but light
that colours you and generates blue cymes.
It's naming things affords me power
to instate empathy.
I need to take you in me and look out
at a blue re-creation,

                              and the shower
proposes meditation.

I transform you to cerulean
and have you speak, it is our way
of individuation, have you think
of why you're here and answerable to death.

The dialogue makes of you what you're not,
rain-sparkling spring-highlight, blown together
so bluely now, forget-me-not.

SUFFOLK NIGHT ARRIVING

Red overhang in blue. The stream's a film
looping beneath an arch.

The nearest house is a white dab
I know is locatable but can't see.
Too many cuts in the sequence.

A pheasant stands on the road. A dead rat
opens its wound to a star. An oak tree

feels for its going leaves.
My nerve-endings flicker for connections

that I can use in the blue night. A car
another car pointing to diverse ways.
The night-film's projected from a dark room.

A white owl bales out stealthily.

BLOOD LINE

Tentative, and by degrees sure at last
it has come home, an animal
chooses to live inside my heart
with all the other hurt creatures
contracted there. They are the ones I let
go out into the world, who couldn't cope
and so return with lesions, scars.
This new one isn't terminal
in its foetal hibernation.
I feel retracted claws, wet fur,

the flicker of two half closed eyes,
china-blue like a kitten's?
Or blood-red? Its stay
might not be long; my poetry
will lead it back into the day
to cross frontiers as an emissary
of words, the lyric flowering as a rose
in a barbed-wire fence.

The creature settles in this month
when hedgehogs go into the dark
caul of zero. The many and the lost
are here with me.
The night comes on the colour of wet bark.

I have my blood line and my dead.
This new one will communicate its dread
in time.
The poem carry it about the world.

CODA

Carlights fire the hill's shoulder.
Around the world my others, friends
direct a luminous river
that feeds us all.
An energized telepathy.
I feel its lightning-flicker
crackle in the hall,
I staying up, sitting up
afraid of myself and the local

blank I've come back to. I can't adopt
a role that fits. I float outside
their fixity, the ones I knew
and now disown as blurs.
Dead arrows on a cloth.
Old shattered trees, a sunken farm,
youth burning up the night
on Japanese bikes. I have lost this place
and found no surrogate
reality. My friends are where
the light touches. I let them in
from London, Amsterdam, Berlin,
arrivals narrowed by a cone
to the immediate. They've crossed
and focus on my need.
The night outside waits like a bear;
I feel the current and anticipate
the river flowing in from everywhere.

TURNING AWAY

I saw you turn your face away
towards a tree, a momentary
act of self-appraisal, a father's doubt
framed by the headlights in the dark,
the motor still running, a moth
caught in the dazzle like a spark

and only guessed the cause for that alarm,
the twist of pain that had you meet
the unconfrontable image

like someone backing from a fire
that reddens on the skin.
The image stayed with me until I came
to invent a double life for you, fraud,
drink or sexual shame?
My own imaginings.

There must have been an owl involved
or earlier its oval shriek
had brought me to the window
still not conscious you were back
from your routinal day,

which later found me imitating you,
meeting your face to turn away.

THE NOVELIST

In his white villa on the Côte d'Azur,
is editing on his word-processor,

routinal tabulations, he is lost
to big money, the gold-fin striking high

against an incandescent azure sky.
Each week he's thrown by a black envelope

which arrives empty, the type-written white
label neatly addressed. If there's a clue

he's dissected the possibilities.
But there are incidents: the swimming pool

disfeatured by oil, the ritual murders
around the coast. He feels his body cool.

Sometimes he thinks someone's inside the screen,
a psychopath banked in its memory,

the tear in words, the masked face showing through
after erasing the chapters on spool,

a white shark surface-streamlined for the kill.
He stops reading. The screen's persistent hum

seems to arrive from space and continue
as a disquieting frequency.

He goes outside; mimosa flourishes.
A youth stands by the gates simulating

fellatio with a pink ice-cream cone,
whoops like an Indian and runs for the sea.

RUNNING WILD

RUNNING WILD

These days we only meet by telephone,
our voices spanning the spaces between:
jets vaporizing crystal arcs, mares-tails
above a sea that's neither blue nor green –

I know its nuances by memory,
so when we speak my visualized backdrop
is of a bay, a dead-drop to the sea,
a lighthouse like a fixed bottle afloat

in a white whirlpool; a place that we've shared
in childhood; and later a drunken rush
across the beach to the car, truancy
from our first shared office our youthful push

to get a handhold on the wheel. Salt-air,
our Bowie car-tape, we were running wild
before we sobered and I went away.
And as we speak, something of the sea's glare

tilts into this room, a window, a glass
destabilizes and a flooding light
falls with a wave's dazzling concavity.
I make believe that spindrift stings my sight;

our words are easy for we've never lost
the correspondence that puts youth in age,
immediacy into recall . . . the gulf
dividing us is one of cloud sculptures

built over thought; and I'll return some day,
that implicit promise, retrieve the past.
We wish that crazily . . . And the weather?
Blue spaces that you love, and here to last.

DANGEROUS

With black clouds building above the city,
the jolts already so interiorized
you risk lifting the tablecloth
to a waterfall's rapid overshoot;
it's nerves you tell yourself, and she,
'imagine we're lost in the Black Forest,
the troops are after us and a gold deer
bolts through interstices before the rain.'
It's 1939 in 1999,
except the piano's different, the jazz
has turned to pure expressionism –
the Blaue Reiter translated into notes.
She slips a silk leg across mine. The sky
is a jet saucer spinning round,
and someone coming from an antiques shop
carries a tiger's head into their car.

'You can't escape from the interior,'
she says; 'I'll place you anywhere I want
with my imagination; where are we
in our relationship?' a saxophone
sounds like a startled forest call.
You place both hands against the wall;
the cold sweat mints. It's 1999.
The rain moves in. We'd like to be alone.
The waitress skips between the packed tables
as though her feet bounced on a ball.

EXECUTIVE

The pace increases; one hand on his head,
the other engaged in semiotics,
his time is molten, wired to the big flash,
he only buys to get above the crash,

his days spent monitoring the walled screens
inside a fish-tank, all reflecting glass
across which clouds smoke, and outside the cars
build to compression, bruised city models

defeated by the endless stop and start.
Who'll get there in the end? If time's money
then it's demythicised of purity,
the gold shower tarnished to chemical rain,

the death-trap tightening around the heart's
cholesterol build, high blood, the burning out
of nerve to accelerate power –
'I'm free to buy and impotent to screw,'

time is the cutting-edge, and after that
death means liquidation . . . But the heat's on,
his thrill is in the moment, achieving
the cheetah's stride that overtakes its prey,

a red stain in the dust . . . The whiskey burns.
He's high on ruthlessness, and shakes the earth
from his air-sealed aquarium.
He'll get there yet – his future contradicts

everyone's; the world shrinks inside his skull,
a miniature he scales truimphantly,
raging his banners' formula –
everything's convertible to money.

HIV FEAR

The intimation, symptomatic threat,
it's of the age and now it's in
the nerves, and I equivocate
over the definitive test,

it can't be me
that's symbiotically
linked to a viral chemistry's
irreversible white-cell march?

the white winter
that brought armies to a numb halt
has transferred itself to the blood.
Ice will immobilize the word,

the line freeze to suspension points . . .
If I'm positive I must
like so many others place a late trust
in antibodies and prepare

to get into myself the way
the green bud tightens in the cold,
compact, centred, withdrawn to find
the light kept burning in the mind

to help with ends and help detach
consciousness from indignity –
the body's dissolution breaking up
into an atrocity.

Fear blacks the corners of the mind,
what do we do to die and how
is it achieved? And will I know
too late to assist others find

a way through that speaks of grace.
We live as we can, who can help
their needs? We hope the end's OK.
We're consciousness still and living today.

FEET ON SHOULDERS

The season multiplies extravaganza;
such pink and crimson peonies heaped in a vase,

and the contained rose turbans, open silks
recalling a Fantin-Latour.

A blue vase on a black lacquered table.
Outside the air is musty with hawthorn,

a slowly assimilated aphrodisiac.
A phallocratic drive works through each tree.

I watch you undress tauntingly,
you balance on high heels in black panties,

a pearl necklace falling to your full breasts,
your body coppered by the sun.

You unclip earrings. The jasmine storms in.
Our window floods with a pink-indigo.

Legs arched, you place your feet on my shoulders,
two satin petals; and we flower as one.

CLEARANCE

Red sunlight picks out letters in the wall;
the crudely hatched interlacing of names
united at that moment in a heart
scratched into granite: Summer '69

Joanna/Dave: the inscription reads still
above the tide-line, compacted glitter
schisted in stone, each wink a mineral.
Their lives and mine? the intersection cuts

obliquely, for I've known this beach
as a sounding-board to each emotion
picked out since childhood; clearance, confusion,
the wave's sky-window lifting to the chin,

concussive fear, the arms striking to reach
a handhold in the surf, the smashed sapphire
running for shore . . . This early evening calm
sets up a contemplative air,

beer-cans, used tubes of Ambre Solaire –
the afternoon's debris awaits the surf,
a random montage pointing. We were here
and left an unconscious exhibit

to comment for us, should we disappear;
and Joanna and Dave, where they are now,
together or apart is speculative,
their names linked in the impulse to survive

a summer's incandescence, keep intact
whatever they knew then and realized
as burning and could qualify
by writing up the inconclusive fact.

RETURNABLE FRISBEE

Leather-backed, upright in a chair, the man
analyses brain-damaged astronauts,
an Otto Dix nose, the contemplative
manner of a green lizard reading faults

in the sunlight, alert to a shadow.
He is a filter, one who redefines
a way of seeing the impossible,
meeting the blindside where the facet shines

and so the planet tilts from dark to light.
How to re-earth, recover gravity,
the body's cycles: **in my dream I walk
and waking float in the enormity** . . .

His blue room's infinite in recession,
multi-dimensionalized like Paul Klee's
ghost-chamber. The mind's outriders
go up as a returnable frisbee.

Sometimes the associations don't meet,
words as experiential signs break down.
A blank mind meets a blank, the troubled fish
are nerve-endings. He looks out over town,

the violet roofs, dark cypress in the park,
and sees a fat man hurrying to meet
a child's orange ball lobbed over the fence,
that spins oddly then settles at his feet.

STAGES

1

The line turns back on itself, figure eight
reversed again when the image shows clear;
the lyric unknotting entanglements
becomes through progress a black chequered snake,

clean and precisional,
triggered to kill.

2

I live with the still uncharted journey.
Artaud falling into aphasia
before touching the shore; the blue island
in mental space.
You read its outline in his dying face.

3

Linear progression. The head swallows the tail,
fellation of metaphor. Where we end
is arbitrary for the narrative's
continuous – the line open
although we never do arrive.
An emerald rainforest, a red sky,
I place them somewhere. Poetry's

like risking a bare hand in a beehive.

RED HOUSE

It stands between a lilac and a grey,
a fixture at the end of town, almost
a film-prop odd amongst untenanted
warehouses, blue thistle-clumps.
                              'Look', they say,
but never really see it, for it's just by chance
it connects with vision, a dream
or trance-state is a surer way
in which to know its location. A red
house painted by Matisse between
a lilac and a grey; at the curtain
a woman looking out, her face
half black, half white, divided equally,
her body too when she turns full frontal.
A second comes to the window,
the fusion of a Swedish blonde and Japanese,
hair split between platinum blonde and black,
and then a German with an Indian.
Here the potential's inexhaustible,

the red house offers alternative lives
to those who would dichotomize
experience and live as two
integrated identities, and they
the clients love two girls at once,
a Balinese, an Italian,
a Greek and a Parisian,

in a red house between a lilac and a grey.

PLAYING TO DIE

He sniffs a line and the world rectifies;
the fine white crystals reinstate his dream
of playing to packed stadia,
his leather body working to entwine
the vertical mike; a lean phallic vine
for whom the hands reach; they would kill to catch
his wasted torso which relies
on speed and over-reach to hit
the high-points with the understated speech
that breaks the lyric, slows the rift
to a subversive questioning, a flit
between two death-states, his hands joined in prayer,
a drug-hooked, narcoleptic exhibit,
pooled by a single red spotlight . . .

Junked by a new decade, his solitary
figure remains indoors; the videos
of his performances screened in each room
renew his resolve to kick the habit.
His fingers on the chords no longer fit
the spacings, and it's someone else's face
stares back from posters – The Black Memory –
live from Australia to the USA.
Disbanded, disillusioned, he's solo
without a record deal and jittery
he's lost it. It's a death-trip anyway.
He's virtuoso in his studio;
they'll find the tapes and resurrect his name,
and burn his body in the halls of fame.

THE GREEN ROOM

We wait for the director. There's no clue
to his identity. We have the script
and vocal cues. A single window's view
admits a dark green sky; a jet's descent
as though suspended in a still-life frame.
There's eight of us and casually convoked
around a table. The one empty chair
is burgundy leather, a circular
device without a back. The rumoured names
turn up imaginary faces; someone
intimates Cocteau's ghost composed of blue
cigarette smoke might blow into the room
and assume recognizable features.
We've learnt our parts. There's nothing more to do.

The red-suited singer angles a boot
on to the table. He is nonchalant
to those on either side of him and drinks
beer from the bottle's neck. There's a tension
that our written instructions over weeks
are print-outs from an automated memory.
We are a play within a play. We're sealed
into the room; security
is likewise automatic. We're nervous
and start to act out roles. The sky stays green.
We sit and wait for what will be revealed.

DE SADE

A grey dress coat, deep orange silk breeches,
a feather in his hat, he's thirty-two.
The château of La Coste is pure gothic.
He wants to socialize aberration,

and have a spiked whip cut her black and blue;
he only ever enters from behind;
a woman's pubis doesn't interest him.
He cuts his flagellant's score into wood

with a sharp knife. Erotomania
will have him savage man or woman, force
his overreach to a dementia
he can't modulate. He finds the body

lacks sufficient points of entry,
he would give it a new geometry
to satisfy his frustration.
After the act there's nothing left to do

but dissociate, work it out again.
At fifty-three his body's new ballast
in prison affords him a pig's belly.
His hair is sand-white, his black coat is torn,

he squats like a toad in his cell
and threatens to expand from wall to wall.
He's found a more protean irritant,
the revisioning of sex word by word,

each close-up magnified by abstention,
for now there's greater elasticity
in the perverse co-ordinates achieved
through the contortions of anatomy . . .

His back supported the Bastille
as a granite turtle-shell. Raging blood.
Free, he ordered baskets of red roses,
sniffed each and trampled them into the mud.

FREE

Looking towards the autumn of the century
that mellow light in which holed windfalls thud
into the grass, yellow and red or green,
and late wasps dazed by alcohol crackle

defiantly, it's quite another state
that we've learnt to anticipate,
not fall, with its natural dissolution
and recovery, but a new season

for which we have no name and imagine
as part of the future, the snow falling
outside a free cinema in Moscow,
two lovers kissing on a fire-escape

in New York, blue flakes dusting her red hair,
a farmer near Stuttgart abandoning
his fields to industry, an autobahn,
and for the last night sleeps with his small herd

in musty stalls. So the human story
we like to think a continuity . . .
21 not 20; and will the change
be like resisting the altitude drop,

as a jet loses height for the airfield?
or be simply like driving fast all night
between two frontiers, and the break of day
finding the driver there, the border-guards

waving him through to breakfast at a farm?
We have to go with it and trust
first footholds are familiar,
before the whirring changes start to spin,

and we, creatures of the old century
might lose our way looking for dead habits –
the things we did and celebrate today,
racing the meadow, thinking that we're free?

SEPARATION

And where we are and how and transitory.
I fix your image so you stay
not jerkily but composite,
a resident of inner space
flashing up in the day's orbit,
leaving me stunned by each new hit

you make with such intensity
I see you as you are moving
into the sunlight, black sweater, blue jeans,
red lipstick and the Javan masks
you wear as earrings,
and I hear your voice
confident in the things you say.
I move my thoughts on your trajectory
and jump at the flashbacks,
the hurt I've caused, the pain
inflicted wrongly from perverse motives.
The wrong I've done that's harmed returns

wringing me out. I lose my way.
I trust in this telepathy,
interiority.
Our dialogue communicates
both love and healing; closes scars.

With me again and always in bright light.
I write and be. You stand inside an arch
at nightfall with the coming stars.

FRENCH POEMS IN THE USA

The wind catches pink roses in her skirt,
a windy snapping across sun-bronzed legs,
crazy uplifting of carmine splashes,
paint that won't stay on a canvas but moves . . .

I read John Ashbery's configurations,
a French poem blown like a wandering kite
across a skyline of white skyscrapers.
Tzara's recklessness couched in the cool ice

prismatically set over Wallace Stevens.
It might be that the poem always needs
an insurance director's strict routine
balanced against the casual: sky-blue jeans,

an easy breathing in of circumstance.
The day's a diamond tropism. And how it shines
glazing the buildings with rococo gold.
Everything seems to move across a screen.

Good poems lift above the century,
the tricolour and stars and stripes combine
in the one vision. Red, white and blue sky vapours
printing their colours in a glass of wine.

EXPECTATION

Timberboard flaking like a silver birch
showing its mottles. Where the wind got in
the rain had followed. Fire charred black deckles

along the wood. For months I wouldn't own
to trespass, but skirted around outside,
convinced the thing could see.
I learnt to hide

in swathes of hemlock umbels, unsurprised
at how a couple stayed in a long time.
Her laughter fanning fire-points in my nerves.
The place compelled and warned me off,
I feared the protean dark inside,

and how any discovery would break
the good thing in me –
childhood's still unrealized expectation.

And when I finally kicked the door to,
the light admitted came from behind me,
tree branches lashed the wall
as confirmation of the illusory
that lived in there and lived in me.

PREPARATORY

He leaves for Mars today, the red planet.
She cooks pasta and reads Pushkin;
he is already programmed for the stars

and hasn't been earthbound for years.
Supernova explosions burn his dreams.
She mind-reads their blue kitten, Ace,
and warms to his electric dimension.
She thinks of failed aspirations. Pasta.
It's an octopus with four hundred legs.
Later an acupuncturist will find
the points that leave her drift downstream –
she floats the Mississippi on her back.

He thinks that he is bound for Mars.
She isn't sure if it's illusory,
except he's preparing for a journey.
His headaches and his sleepwalking,
an orbital somnambulist?
Last month he sleepwalked for a day
down to the coast. His skin is turning black.

Her day is busy. Drinks, a Sci-Fi film;
at nine, her mutant lover. Pasta first.
She looks down. There are claw marks on her wrist.

IT MUST BE

The sky's a lilac tent. He goes outside
and listens for a car. A greenish bird
he hasn't seen before lies buckled, dead,
its slashed wing pinions open like a fan.

The hills insulate him; they're touched up red
and correspondingly estrange. His eye
takes in so much today: solid colour,
a mobile of pink clouds. What's in his head

is different from the world outside. His ear
is trying to create the valley roar
of dust that reverberates in the hills
from her punchy accelerator kick

after the last spiral bend, the floored oak,
the raunchy music from her stereo
filling the gaps. Her dark glasses, her hair
streaming in the blowback, her crazy yelp

at slamming dead are things he's come to know.
The outside's different though. It's tomorrow
pretending to be today – or ten years
before he earthed out here from the city;

the aircraft passing is so ponderous
it seems fixed in space. He stubs at the ground,
and watches a convoy of ants search out
the flaws in the dead bird. What if he takes

the garish body inside, places it
beside a heaped fruit-dish, a cobalt jar
and paints its still-life decomposition.
He thinks of that, but looks out for the car,

impatient, living now for her return,
the vacuous sky suddenly too big,
the world around him odd, and where the light
catches the high ridges they start to burn.

THE RECOLLECTION

A square black door opening into the sun,
it seemed like that, or an eclipse at noon,
an interference in the galaxies,
a sun-spot, particle so magnified,
its drift entered my focus – the white beach
stretched taut by surf, the shallows a green moon
tilting through waves, diffused, fragmented, clear,
the midday burning, and it threw me wide,
this deepening accompanied by a shout,
as though someone was drowning, going down –
mouth, nose and eyes, the right arm struck
a last time above the water.
No movement on the beach; the couples tanned,
or sat under umbrellas looking out
at a seamless block of lapislazuli.
It seemed impossible someone should die
so near, so many eyes, the inshore craft
rounding the coast from a harbour;
and yet I sat up tense and felt the spin
of a presentiment move through my head,
its irreversible momentum hit
with so lasting an aftermath, the light
turned silver, black then red,
and cutting through the blue surface I saw,
a flexing, black, triangular shark's fin.

RETURNING TO PRINT

The black arm wavers on its numeral.
Time and its fractional divisions stay

outside his blood. It is a different day
inside, making the pieces fit and where

an oblong red balloon floats in the blue pool
is one caption in the diffuse glitter

of images. The things he reads restart
through open vowels their tiny blood-red hearts,

each character's alive to exercise
on the imaginative trampoline,

and then returns to print, a burial
within closed covers. Now he draws the blinds

and cool fingers diffuse body-lotion
into his frame. The girl is pantherine,

green-eyed. His torso is a light canoe.
The novel floats with him. He starts to shine.

AWAY FROM IT ALL

The rain breaking quite suddenly across
a swirl of poplars painted by Soutine? –
it had to be like that, the transition
snappy and lucent, while the blue road shines

with promise of a future. Who were they
the three drinking wine beneath a bulk oak,
she dressed in black leather, two in bright suits,
composed on a cloth when the shower broke

their quick sequence of photographs? They ran,
and remember the afternoon for that,
and more for leaving than their heady stay,
will speak of it later grouped in a flat;

the violet sky, the convertible soaked,
the dash to reposition the sun-roof,
and something in the downpour, silvery,
cleansing, seeming to point towards a truth

there for the knowing in their exposure
to elemental change; his gold wristwatch
blurred by the streaming droplets, linen suit
turned wet and baggy, his friend there to catch

his fallen wallet on the run. They'll speak
of it later as unremarkable,
an afternoon torn at the seam and how
squirrels dropped to their improvised table,

and how the action resembled a film,
a spontaneous cut, the girl lifted high
between two men in white suits, losing shoes,
balanced a moment as though she would fly.

EXTENDED DAYS

A burnished pink light; the long summer stays
as a gold membrane silked by the first leaves;
letters gilt-blocked into the sky –

We'd like to stay always.
The summer people won't be gone this year;
the sunning girl turns over on her face
to feel the heat imprint itself,
a triangle from an all-over tan.
Silence extends to the corners of space.

The music reaches me, 'People are Strange',
Jim Morrison's posthumous voice arrives
as though he still lived on the air.
Once it was heard on beaches in LA
as something urgently contemporaneous
with living *then* as *now*.

Every direction leads to the blue sea.
The names are heard, Lucinda, Ciona,
perpetuation of the myth
that girls step out of the sun.

I wait by the sea-stairs and look into
a lazy distance. The wave spreads a shawl;
and if fall comes will red clouds drop like leaves
parachuting slowly out of the blue?

THE CATCH IN THE STAIRS

It caught us out, the unexpected gap
in a deserted lighthouse; its rusty spiral stair
severed, stove in by boulder-heads
that vandals brought to it. Half up, half down,
our momentum returned on itself
as though our minds had gone up to the top
and blindingly returned. Hoarse gulls somewhere,
and further out a swagging blue-green sea.
We climbed backwards into the tilting light,
recalling other stairs, marble, granite,
treacherous, rimed sills leading from a wharf
one night in Venice, the vaporetto
audibly bisecting canals. Distance
created by that sound. And others too;
your leading me up a vertical flight
in a tight skirt to an attic studio,
and coming down barefoot, afraid to fall.
We've found our balance on so many gradients,
one foot forward, one back, or suspended
between decisions, meeting up again
to find a level in the sunlit hall.

BLUE AND BLACK ALTERNATIVES

Colour additives recompose the scene,
a switch to blue and black and it's five years ago,
you're looking out at a black ragged cloth
that won't stabilize on the blue sky face,
and that red splash looks like a glass of wine
thrown into an indefinite suspension.
Two people discourse on the beach;
they're unperturbed by the storm energy
which casts a shadow round them like a cloak.
She skimps a white top over full-blown breasts,
and neither rise from a spread violet towel.
We stay behind glass, cut off from the world,
our own sound-system falsifies what's real,
music in our interior,
taking our thought-waves somewhere else. Snow owls
sitting in that black sky might complement
the surreal composition. They wrestle.
The storm delays and seems to pass over,
vague columns of rain dispersing at sea.
We stayed, hands and faces pressed to the glass;
disappointed the climax never came,
watching the couple entertain renewed sunlight;
her top removed again. The day the same.

VISUALS

THE ONE

You could be anywhere –
the wind snapping a black scarf in your hair,
a spine-split book of poetry
in a greatcoat pocket,
walking the winter streets of Manhattan,
or on a surf-thrashed beach in the Camargue,
hipbones pronouncing a black bikini,
Cap Ferrat, Biarritz, Copacabana –
always the same inimitable beauty,
followed but never turning round
to own to an identity.

I've searched for you through so many cities,
giving back what you offer me –
the gift of poetry,
words answerable to your elusive
neither-here-nor-there anonymity –
a face amongst the crowds,
mouth open to catch snowflakes, or naked,
emerging from a violet sea
to roll in a red towel. I sit and wait
for your appearance, that's more frequent now
in the advancing century.
I contemplate crossing the new threshold
with you – two pinpoints on the brink of space
running to meet the continuity . . .

MAGENTA DRAPES

Bonnard would have moved mauve to the foreground
and placed his hectic reds where space recedes
to a tenuous distance. It is right
he throws us by disorientation,
no hooks to the familiar; the shock
upending. And the world's like that,

an unlearning of what we think we see
tented by shadow, proved by light.
That time I saw you on the unlit stair,
I on the third floor out of four,
you in a cobalt suit with blueblack hair,
on your way down, you'd given up on me,
we passed each other without knowing it,
each concentrating so exclusively
the image had absorbed the reality
of meeting. We were ourselves, somewhere else.
And going up, you opening out the door
to a white studio with purple chairs,
a dull pink, primed canvas still half complete
in its abstract portrait called 'What you See
Isn't the Sum of It', a vase, a hand,
fragmentary things, a head without a face
emerging from purple drapes, while a train
quite leisurely goes off into the sky
towards a cloud which might even mean rain.

EXTRAORDINARY

I place jet earrings on the table sphinx.

Extraordinary how reading poetry
is like stripping a girl to black panties
a sunflower between her legs

Breton, Desnos and Ashbery –
a bite into the marvellous

tasting like quince, black figs, pine on the sea.

AMAZEMENT

A red-headed girl in a field of sunflowers
under a black sky sits down and listens
to the print-out of her thoughts.

She's come across an invented country,
it's like a painting and she's lost somewhere
within the fictional. She turns around

expecting to find Manhattan
on the skyline, a Jumbo losing height,
a pinkish haze diffused above buildings.

A novel's being disclosed in her head;
the flashes crystallize in stills.
Her skin turns silver; she floats through the air

and slows, to find the landscape altered:
a blue plain extends to a circular
moon-shaped building, lit up, glass floor by floor.

She walks towards it, and looks back again,
her old familiar New York is gone.
The plain is glass, a deep prismatic floor

through which she sees boats on a green river,
and helicopters twinkling above town.
She knows the race of new women

are in the lunar building and prepares
to take her part in their coming
to rule the moon-instructed centuries.

ABSENT DAY ABSENT TIMES

Most days I'm conscious of the sequential –
the hours I fill are me, it's me who lives
inside the words, typing, or walking round
keeping an eye on the world, finding out
the right particular: first snowberries,
a white shirt's mimetics hung up to dry,
a Mondrian poster of a red cloud
seen through an open window, or a girl
hair tented in an orange towel,
snapping shut the green louvres of a blind.
There's music too: a Chopin nocturne alternates
with what is new in pop, hitting the street.

But these are days which I don't recognize,
hours which are purposeful but slip outside
control, I have the consciousness
of what I'm doing but the detour takes
me into side-streets, shops or cinemas
to dilute too great an intensity.
White hours, white days as though a mist blanked out
recall; I found myself climbing the stairs
to a bridge above a disused rail-line,
blackberry bushes crowding willow-herb,
my hands going wide of a hold on things,
and yet I needed to be there
unconsciously, and later made my way
back through familiar streets to a café,
confused by time, my disorderly hair,
my wallet lost, my fountain pen, my rings.

CONTINENT OF SCULPTURES

When I returned from somewhere with no name,
I had to communicate its reality
like Marco Polo trying to engage
a corresponding imagination,
a purple mind able to think a sea
as vitrified and over which great water-spiders swarmed
in a continuous pattern of lace;
a map of emerald and turquoise silks.
I'd come from the continent of sculptures
and seen the deformations, incongruities,
the square heads, oval physiognomies,
bodies left as sarcophagi,
blond hair on a marble head, red on jet,
and the sexual impossibilities,
someone with a stone penis in their ear,
facing a woman without legs,
and on her brass face a bright tear
which wouldn't dry; a glittering aigrette.
Truncations, elongations, a living city
created by Picasso, Brancusi,
Giacometti's anorexic line.
And who would believe the transformation?
A glass sea, a red potato-shaped moon
like Phobos rising above Mars,
a sky of planetary irregularities,
fish and birds in the air, and my returning here
with news that change is on the way,
a stone finger and thumb as evidence
I made the journey, got here in a day,
three stone toes acting as a surety.

PICKING UP

I thought the day was a painting:
white cubic buildings across the river,
a yellow ferry working in that space,

wind on the water like shot taffeta.
The nearer I came the further things were.
It's all happening in another town.

You get in close and there's a rooftop crowd,
silver and gold dresses, the men in black.
Down in the street a hearse attracts the eye

of a girl with a leopard on a leash.
Someone points out a street which disappears.
They're shooting a film in the sky.

A second ferry crosses the divide,
aimed for the side I'm on – I'm over there
I tell myself, central to things.

And other visuals attract;
an ad-balloon, a giant blue umbrella
promoting a film: Diamonds in the Rain.

I'm bilocated. A is B: B A.
The blue arc of sky above the river
is shot with a black wedge of hurried geese.

WAYS THERE

The red birds sit on black buildings
the red buildings overshadow black birds.
I saw them in a town I once passed through

and re-encountered as experience
I have with you. You call me upstairs to untie
your silk ribbons. Outside blue feathers fall
into the fields, into my poetry.
Blue feathers fall from a blue sky.
The poem that I'll write shows through
in fragmentary hieroglyphics, its speed
too fast to slow into focus.
It overshoots the lights on the airstrip.

You teach me to forget the afternoon
and my appointment with the real.
The red and black town re-routes in my head,
hooded figures step from an arch.
My orgasm in you lights up a moon.

WINTER CREATURE

Think of the wind anatomized. A North
or East containment of that energy,
a giant bear risen out of the ice
to systematically fell forests, uproot farms,
turn cars back by presentiment
it rules the road. Its eyes are two green stars.
Its nuclear core means fission;
the advent of a white winter

if it breaks free. I hear cars in the street;
white against white in crisp-packed snow,
headed for points of reference in a night
that burns through a central window;
the cosmos looking at the universe
that's lit below.
                        Kafka is walking home
in the wrong century.
He leaves no footprints. He is still followed.

If there are wolves they've entered our cities
unnoticed; they brush at our legs
in supermarkets; a police-van
is flattened to a tin can
by a bear materialized from a building.
Kafka doesn't look round.

I open a curtain on the morning.
A starfish of ice occupies the glass.
Part of the landscape's disappeared.
It went without a sound.

SEEING

Wind in the dark blue casuarina pines.
A cloud-house, white vapour blocks built in air,
stands in blue space above the sea.

A change in atomic structure and this sea-lily
might be a torrent, and the horse
a circular disc spread over the field.

I walk the afternoon to think these things
into happening; sandgrains burn my feet
from their compacted heat.
I seem lighter for wishing to change shape;
the place I aim towards seems to retreat.
I'll never reach the rocky overhang.

Light has established white pillars. The bee's
a jerky black spot to the eye.
Someone stands up in a gold bikini,
blinding me with a sequin-hurricane.

ASYLUM

A brickish-blue sky. Yellow laburnums.
A few inmates drag round the asylum garden.
Red hair, green eyes, I imagine Van Gogh
on such a day at St Paul's,
torn coat, knobby boots, seeing everything
in flames, seeing clean through a wall.

I could have walked the other way,
but fascination draws me here. The mad
have gone a stage further than most would dare.
We'd like to interchange with them,
receive their visions through an ordered mind.

Cows munch in a nearby meadow. A parked red car.

I'm here and I have come this far.

MIRÓ

A visual transparency, an exuberant
metamorphic fluidity of signs:-
and colour, how that swims through primary
creations, aphids, tadpoles, stars,
a scarlet and black kite, green and yellow
fish-shapes, volutes, snails, shells,
and everything sings 'we are becoming
the forms you see', the constellated figurations
that once lived inside and are free
to challenge in their hectic liberation.
And woman's central to the orgasmic suns and moons
describing eccentric orbits –
black suns, a black woman risen at dawn,
one half of the globe scarlet. How space fills
with your implosive progeny,
cellular, ovoid, and how they geometricize
spatial planes, and the morning star
brings with it the vibrational resonance
of a frantic cosmos, bird, spider, fish and mask
are part of the catastrophe,
they've gone to reach the light but it is black.
Your lyric is affirmative –
it grows into a cosmos: we watch it flicker
alive with its multiple antennae:
not one of your creatures ever turns back.

WHY ARE WE HERE? WHO ARE WE? WHERE DO WE GO?

A painting by Gauguin

I close my eyes to see. The primitive
arrests Gauguin; the dark increases light.
A brush and crude piece of burlap
await his vision, and bold orange nudes
are offset by blue and Veronese green.
Who are we? and how pensively
the ripe Tahitan women feel the split
between luxurious fertility –
nature that lives only to proliferate,
and the black seed that grows into a death
inside the body.
                            How can it happen to me?
and those I love? And is there no return
to picking red fruit from the tree,
children, animals, a community,
fierce love at night, a lacquered turquoise sea,
scents, tastes and sounds, and if not, why were we
granted the little that we know?

Oceania. And the blue idol stands
beneath a tree. If there's a poetry
that affirms question as the will to live
beyond life and death as the same,
then it's confirmed by the self-questioning
of these grouped women; it's in all of us
the need to find through doubt a clear
apprehension of who we are,
lifting our death up high until it shines
bright and companionable as a fixed star.

BALCONY OVER EUROPE

He stands on a balcony high over Europe,
a Western capital, the dark blue sky
printed with rose-coloured clouds, and swallows
are flying. He dreams of increased vision,
a plane of light set like a window in his view,
that magnifies the universe, takes in
the land masses until the blue
of sea and sky predominate.

                                              Scarlet

geraniums and white petunias
show in window-boxes and opposite
a girl pads round in a transparent bra,
fishing for accessories; one black stocking, two . . .
Another window is a studio
in which the artist imposes
aerial perspective on the capital
and works in greys, yellows and blues.

He waits a long time under the cloud-change,
detached, while the recognizable day
pursues its busy, inconclusive ends.
On the outskirts of town, the pines begin
to thicken in their density,
a blackish-green solidarity,
cool in its grouping, and his eye rests there.
He brings a chair out, it's his lazy way
of lifting things out of the ordinary.

APOLLINAIRE

It's raining calligrammes over Paris,
over Le Pont Mirabeau, Rue Christine,
eyelets and tadpoles shimmer on the glass.
The cars are beetles polished by the rain;
blueblack, bottle-green, crimson, bronze,
milling to open up.
                              Someone's reading
Les Onze Mille Vergers, a dark mouth
like Marie Laurencin, crushed carnation,
but not her Creole hair, green almond eyes,
a student looking in through a window,
perhaps envying the formative years
of the new century, Matisse, Picasso, Braque,
the implosive holocaust, visual news
of the immediate, and that round man,
Guglielmo de Kostrowitzky –
Guillaume Apollinaire, his pear-shaped head,
Chaplinesque expression, childish, obscene,
reading his poems without removing
a pipe, clownishly-sad and bibulous,
walking all day and night across
the city, finding a voice for poetry,
plaintive as rain falling on white lilac,
or urgent with the fragmentary
ellipses of speed, ending up trepanned,
the green myth of the posthumous . . .

The rain gives over. A blue afternoon
arrives and dazzles; the girl makes to leave,
places the book in her bag, the logos
shining like traffic-lights on each black sleeve.

ROMANCE

We missed the chance or was it over-reach,
corrected by each new impulse the risk

affords, the afternoon open
like a convolvulus, a funnelled throat

trapping desire, we're led right to the rim,
so many faces, musicality

of bodies, and that crimson heart-shaped mouth
evokes Paul Klee's figure, the mourning child

dancing with a peacock's feather . . .
The eye can read into its captive finds

the impossible plurality
of loves we never could contain –

this girl's green eyes, the other's shapely legs,
the one with nipples like mauve fuchsia buds

pressed against disarming chiffon,
and more than that, the summer day itself,

alluringly provocative,
an aphrodisiacal rose-crater,

vibrant, burning, promising wildfire nights,
the gain we held, the shooting-star we lost.

BETWEEN THE 3RD AND 5TH

Our meeting came by accident,
exchange of eye-beams and improvident
to immediate fulfilment. 'Two years',
you said, 'and meet me on a bridge
above the river, the 3rd and 5th, and I'll be there
awaiting you.' I watched you disappear
out of the café door, black hair, red coat,
a Japanese face, small red mouth,
but tall and leaving on the air
an unidentifiable perfume.

I lived with your image in mental space
and tried to draw your resistant features
imagining you jetsetting from place to place
or looking over a lover's shoulder
into our projected future,
the lamps on bridges all over Europe
clearing the bluish haze, a white ferry
lit up as a restaurant,
my returning at hourly intervals
with eyes searching the face of each stranger,
apprehensive, prepared to stay. 'I'm here
between the 3rd and 5th. I walked out
on my life for you; the black river
couldn't care less. In my country
the harvest is one of abundant grapes.
I've written you into a book. I fear . . .'

And now the summer's burnished. I prepare
in my mind for your arrival,
stone lions watching, a blue in the light

picking out red and gold, finding your hair's
divide at the crown – will it be like that
tied up, wind-blown, a black coat not a red
hurrying through the capital
before the last swallow, the early night.

OFFICE TO STATION

It's down to time and its cross-references,
and how the royal-blue delphiniums
match your silk blouse, your geranium-red hair
lifting the street in your pronounced stiletto walk
from an office to a station.
Always at the still end of afternoons,
it's you arrest my vision, down to finding out
a red bra strap unconsciously
slipping a shoulder. And in the gold light
it's André Breton's Paris peregrinations
come to mind, the eye hunting for the coincidental
image it's conceived, then transferring to
girls in constricted skirts, an orange sun.
An hour to re-charge poetry
and retrieve your feminine ostentation,
which has me think of sunflowers, marigolds,
solar explosions, poems by Lorca.
My eye holds you until you disappear
into the crowds, my words finding embodiment
for you, in the fevered, high-summer, heady air.

THUNDER RAIN

The warm thunder rain arriving at dawn
scores loudly in the purple copper-beech,
and has us rise to face a bronze electric sky,
our pores breathing after oppressive heat,
the journey in a car's tin-trap
that brought us here feverish, bugged, dead-beat,
simmering for the coast's stupendous surf,
the sky's vaulted, empty green frame,
the future out there as an abstract designation,
a star-map or a diagram
still unlocated. Match a yellow pear
with a red apple on a black backcloth
and we've achieved the possibility
of marriage? It's the cubic air
we unite with the sea, such possibilities
of living free. Our nerves are badly scorched;
the lightning's fangs illuminate
our dark-room questions; will the negatives
survive the process, the final spotting
omit the flaws?

We open the window
on long marching rains that dazzle the coast,
smoke in their bounce-back off the street,
and feel cleansed by the storm, its healing glow,
the apple-coolness to the linen sheet.

CHANGE OVER

The cat fixes the world with two green moons
contracted by the light to jasper slits.
The day I'd thought was just the day outside
has shifted out of focus like a still.
Magritte would have conceived this. I can see
the opposite street removed to a hill;
the houses drunk on their pink reflections
float out into extended planes. The gap
is a glass lake, and if I walk across
its surface, will I find the same faces
at windows, and a continuous map
without a flaw, the ordinary world
about its functions? The daily spaces

by which I locate externals are lost.
If I am seeing through a dream prism,
then there's no fade. My blue cat hooks a moth
and tears a silk wing from its fuselage.
A time-warp, fissure? I lift a black cloth
from the back window, and again it's changed –
the garden with its apple tree is now
a concrete landscape and square warehouses
are featureless constructs, built to conceal
things of which I'm instinctively afraid.
There's nothing there I recognize. The sun
is dark green, obscured by its dusty rays.
And perhaps it's like this. The end we fear
as sudden, nuclear, burning our days
with fall-out, occurs as a transition
in time and space, a dream landscape that stays
to have us claim it a reality,
adjust, acclimatize, and venture out
to see what we have lost and what we've won.

SNAPS

It is a war-film and he runs away
into the autumn forest; stags are there
in pouring leaf, such gold and red
he thinks of wine, a district in the Loire,
a girl waiting for him if she's not dead,
a mother pulling warm hen's eggs
out of the straw. But it's a different day,
his defiance, his liberty
have opened up another space. He's stepped
outside time; he is hunted now
for going free, and tears at ripe berries
to assuage an irate hunger.
His hands, his feet, suddenly don't belong
to anyone he's known. The deer retreat.
Their wet black eyes are disengaged from war.

He doesn't know what region or country
he's fetched up in. He's cooked in dirt.
If there is an eye watching him,
it will run over his anatomy
like a lover who prizes a body
before he kills. He walks into cover.
It's dark inside and smells of earth.
If people came here once they went away
in their own time. He needs to find a stream,
a barn, bury himself in straw.
He goes on hallucinating and CUT
a woman in the ditch is giving birth . . .

APARTMENT

They sit. One polishes a red apple,
admiring as he does the yellow streaks
the light elucidates. He's got it now
to the right consistency, a hard shine
presented to the palate. The other
sits looking out of the window
at a green sky. They're waiting for a third?
and on the table a tape-recorder's
loaded with a blank cassette. A press-suite?
The room has three black leather chairs, white walls,
a turquoise Hockney print, and on the floor
a rectangular box that's wrapped in gold;
a gift-wrapped present? There's no sound at all:
their voices have cut out and words rejoined
the uncharged grouping of cells in a hive.
No crackle, just the welling up of thoughts
into random release. Who will arrive?

The blond one charts the brief course of a plane
above the city, and where it recedes
he meets the vanishing point of his thought,
a frontier in the sequence. He startles.
The other one snap-lights a cigarette.
His black hair swishes. It is glossed like silk.
Neither looks up at a knock on the door,
nor confers. They remain silent. A red
warning light flashes once and then goes dead.

EROTICA

THAT SUMMER

A red lion entered your dreams.
Polio in the water, torrid dust
and a nightingale in the eucalyptus.
You reading the Greek anthology
all these years and sea-storms later.

Who will hear us through?
What we've known, written and read
burns with a transparent flame.
Your intruder was sun-faced, red.

Night measured by throaty cries.
Toenails clawing a thin wall,
silken legs gone up so high.
Fierce love scales a ladder;
our red-headed intruder
burnt eye-holes in the night.

Villages lost to hills.
The sea in the sky is blue glass;
the poem fragments split
like mineral from a rock.

We stayed a month. The lion wouldn't go.
Your see-through red nightie
was clear as a window,

ravaged by the lion's paw.

LOVE IN THE AFTERNOON

The louvres on the Venetian blinds snap shut,
phasing out a beach-scene, a turquoise sea,
the beach-guards' improvised fibre-glass hut,

fronting the cadenced surf, and by the quay
the black hotels coffined against the sky,
the burnt-sienna cliffs, a momentary

blue needle-frieze slatting into a dark
that's intimate. We've tented out the day,
our early explorations in a park

have brought us back to your hotel not mine.
Your skirt is pinched down like a second skin,
a sort of shedding as you curve your spine,

your amber flush without strap marks, your round
bottom visible through transparent net.
You bend down low. Your hair streams to the ground.

We're like a summer storm. Our bodies meet
in crazy hurricanes of fantasy
and what your hands don't supplement, your feet

find ways to do; we are a geometry
so oiled and intermeshed we've adopted
in one figure a new anatomy,

a sinuous fluency, while outside
a heat-struck afternoon has swimmers run
in ones and twos to meet the rising tide.

PURPLE BANANA

Her finger trick creates a banana:
it is ophidian how he erects
and telescopes into her lipsticked pout
and undulates a slow motion
in and out, not a sixty-nine,
she crouched down on her haunches, bottom up
in air-sheer white panties.

She imagines a tongue teasing her crack
and he additional fingers on his balls,
they need inventives to participate
in sensory extravagance;
the weird conjunction of geometries,
two side by side, one flipped over,
the other on his back.

He eases his purple banana free
before it shoots its seeding galaxy.
Fellatio as an aperitif
stimulates the volcanic impetus
to other pleasures.

                              She ascends a scale
of excruciating laughter;
it's guesswork what he does to her
and where he is and over and over
their tensions twist around a molten core.

WEEKEND

Big blue hydrangeas stare through the window,
their colour addressing a green sunset.

You sit in a black turban hat, naked
except for black stockings, a spotted tie.
The overblown roses in the tumbler
excoriate vermilion scrolls.
An aircraft tail-flashes into the dusk.

A prelude to the wired disconnections
that find a meaning in Bartók.
You settle down to watch the evening in,
the light lifting with it a lake
into a focused luminosity.
A garden wall, a cherry tree;

and beyond that the big conspiracy
stretching away
with red tail-lights sparking a motorway.
You wriggle silk toes. We are here to stay.

BIKINIS

And who's the girl? so sinuously oiled,
no backstrap, facedown on an orange towel,
her black bikini bottom a sharp V,

minimal, arresting; the eye takes in
the body as an exhibit,
beauty the way we'd know it as the hand
appraises what sight singles out,
affirms its contour, looks for the divide
pronounced in the material.
Beach-spotting, here the Latin blond
is rivalled by the South American,
the Cretan abandoned to the sungod's
pressurized energy. Heat and more heat.

Girls loved more for what they conceal
in red and white or blue and black,
curvy, inviting to the eye,
fig-ripe, mythic in unattainability –
I watch the first run topless, reckless, fast
into a cerulean sea.

PLAYING WITH FIRE

You going down, contortionist
to give me head with pink lipstick,
a black girl with red hair,
your face a locket. A green curtain drawn
on the afternoon rain.

Your vibrations drew the volcanic core
to a white tributary of fire
eased out as pearls.
Your drop-earings shook
diamante flashes, two waterfalls
responsive to your rhythmic tongue,
you lying in a black g-string,
conical breasts with nipples
like purple anemones.

I came, imagining seraglios
and all the positions that we'd achieved,
the best one, your legs right over your head
in a three-quarters somersault,
I straddling as though suspended
in taking off into a gymnast's vault.

SENSUALITY

Biting a half-moon from a scented peach,
its red dusky skin clinging like a dress,

is to observe how its pronounced cleavage
induces tangy referents, retrieves

visual awareness of the marks I left,
little areolas on either side

of your divide. High summer's green silk tent
of leaves is like a river in the air,

it smells of orange, lime. Your scarlet lips
are two canoes, one floating upside down

in a glass cave. I point into their heat
and think of warm springs rising in the hills.

My tongue settles on yours, a corolla
contained within an arched calyx; our hands

point to erotic keyboards, how the back
and sides resonate, we are riding surf

on an imaginary board, our legs
grow to a single vine patterned with leaves.

I enter you as a full peony
whose petals close over my laval stream.

UNDERCURRENTS

1

They converse in the stairwell. It is late.
He might have blown the other, zipped him up,
and now the altercation, the flawed date,

the impresario's tamed falsetto,
the grab at leather under a nursed light,
muted recriminations. One must go

after the risk, the bolting of a door,
back into the night: red and green twinklings
lighting the port, and up on the fourth floor

a lamp extinguished. The small incident
carries, is transmitted to other minds
who build a narrative from the event,

diversifying context. Was it that?
a pick-up who was desperate, a blood-spot;
the hunted one now downstairs in his flat?

2

The issue's always unresolved.
He's married and walks back through streets.
His life is like a bookmark in the night's
open fiction, a red braid showing dawn
above the harbours. It's the undertow
threatens, the altogether blacker pool
in which his emotions feed.
                              Now he stands,
resting against the sea-wall. Heavy surf
breaks on this side, a fomenting dazzle
pushing a stone necklace across the sand.

3

The dream-book's written and we're all in it,
only we'll never live to reach its end
or know where it begins. Others live us,
extending possibilities
to how the action's never localized,
but diversified into the story.

It happened once, but these are variants –
the slow-exposure flash revealed a face
preoccupied by inner space;
the images connecting with a page
we'll never read. It's turned over each night
by the archival myth that rules the stars,

and we wrote it, the continuity.

THROUGH AND OUT

THE VOWEL-GOD

The treeline's a jaguar's launched trajectory
suspended in its leap: the movement holds
then whistles back to equipoise.
I crouch here listening to that pine-green sea,
trying to shape words to a geometry
that liberates them from the preconceived
structure of a morphology
the eye's come to anticipate. The door
is in the page and opens to transparency,
the word-shaper sculpted from light,
guards the entrance to space, little vowel-god
with Krishna's blue feet and a sphinx's quizzical
sun-face, receptive to experience
language can't get through to the other side,
and accepting the poem as a bride
to be led to the inner chamber, heaped
on silk cushions for the union.
Her body's clear through white translucency.

The wind runs again: shadows whip the page,
the sound turned off. If I look to the hill
the sunlight is a bird's gold wings
cutting through green. I need to find the door
and go to the interior.
I'm wanted on the inside where the work
is consummated, and the vowel-god shows
his feet as an azure tablet.
The poem's fluent there; its meaning sings.

THROUGH AND OUT

A door into the trees. It was a location
to find amongst bottle-green pines
a diffused light,
a way into the interior, and out
again into a different day – deeper

for having lived through that green density.
The way was through the bottom of the sea
and up a slope towards a car
parked off the road.
The sunlight on it like a star.
The journey solitary.

I came out questioning identity,
marked by the change; I'd done it once before,
and caught the sunbeam on the needled floor.

GETTING THERE

The image deepens of you as you were.
I think back to that jetty-afternoon,
a keel swimming in clear water,
a detached, sculpted reflection,
beamed curvature.

Just a small harbour with its lobster boats
packed with orange marker floats,
blackbacks vigilantly raucous for fish,
the waves still measuring out history . . .

We'd parked the car and followed to the sea,
an open chapter or a closed
dependent on our reading. A marine
prospect of greenish-tourmaline.
The place seemed to have been waiting for us.

It was a tincturing. We knew it then
in how our confusion came clear
for looking into water.
Brightness entered; a new lucidity.

It precipitated our coming together,
two at the jetty's end, the sea
a chameleon like memory.

THIS YEAR

Everywhere blue delphiniums.
It seemed a name to cling to and a blue
reminder of high summer.

Too conscious of impermanence,
I felt the shadow net your flesh. A cloud
sat in the room awaiting Buñuel
to rehearse its part in the film.

That summer we read only Ashbery
and lived inside his narratives.
Imagination as a modern allegory,
the voice taking up with the part.

Bees blackened in the white clover;
your red brush snapped the voltage from your hair.

We tried to make believe this was our time,
this year, not next, and how they swarmed our clothes,
the little flowers from the lime.

NIGHT LIGHT

A light in a sleeping house:
a yellow rectangle we remember
driving through unrelieved dark, blueblack planes

that give like a window which doesn't break,
self-multiplying barriers that afford
imaginary opposition to speed;
that light catches, the one whose solitary

marches with words or listens to a radio
bring the word through spaces to where
he sits watching for the first green flare
above a mountain. Frozen stars.

We travel with it, an illness or death,
or simply a mind that over-reaches
oneiric tributaries, red tigers
surrounding a house without walls . . .

That light burns in and adds a dimension
to the continuous journey.
It won't go out until the day
it's used in a poem, when a new dark
with one light out will come to stay.

NIGHT

Star-shine. Again you answer configurations
conceived in inner space, meeting out there
the abstract drift, the mineral cells

within you, nebulae, transmitted codes.
Night again. Black marble,
obsidian, the poem's twisted shriek
forming a paper-heart
to be nailed on a tree
and splashed with blood from the owl's killing. Night

as a terminal to which we return,
standing in a place where the wind's trapped high
                                             among trees,
a space between winds, and the stars brighter
for the sky's clarity.

Two join together to celebrate night.
The elegy begins again.
Words black with praise, minted with light,

and later, a moving pillar of rain.

SOMETHING ELSE

The man's a messenger, a psychopomp,
if you detach him from the crowd and freeze
him in the white light equalized at noon
above this beach, a dark blue sea
so cool it's lapidary,
and follow him up off the dusty path
to where a beach-hut affords shade, you'll find
his interest in the white interior
suggests a hermeneutics of the soul,
an abstract geometry made transparent
by his discovery
of living with a dimension brought right
and honeycombed into the sphere
that admits a completion somewhere else
in azure light planes. He's progressed too far
for you, and has you know it by a smile,
a loosening of clothes without provocation
to show the singular blue star
written into his diaphragm. He'd have you stay,
but he is something else and the beach road
points back through pines to the lazy blue bay.

THE SYSTEM

The spider trembles in its fine snowflake,
attuned to pure vibration like the stars.
The individual's like that,
a note so sensitive that if it breaks,
the damage is recorded by the light
and stays there as a scar, a black thumb blur.

The system's mixer bites like a sausage machine.
New age automatons fan out.
I watch a young man sitting with his back
to concrete, playing a guitar
in slashed denims. The real have no money.
The poet, thinker, street junkie,
looking into a different sun,
the drop-out from the bureaucratic claw

hold good against the law,
and touch upon the hope of being free.

PASSING

You huddled into black, the breath in you
singing the poem to a tall stemmed flower
issuing from your throat.

Day is it, night is it? unrecordable time
with the simple things that come great
from divining the inner.
You nearer
for showing like that, fingers expressive
of jewels, rhythm, instructing
the dance of words like the wind

parting leaves in the cherry.
You must read me again how beginnings
unfold into myths that gather like vultures
searching for ends

in their way, in all possible futures.

THE WORK AND PATIENCE

The Alpine road followed the valley down
to a river-bed of blue gentians.
The sky a dark ultramarine, thin air

to crystallize the living verb.
Angels were in this light,
slow dazzle leaving no shadow
on the page at Muzot,
the hands asking
the collection of cold flame
and in the going
absence left like a scent
of rose smelt from a window
overlooking pink and scarlet
tumbling summer roses.

The work and patience;
we are never nearer
the source, nor in it,
but a transient deepening
registers, recordable
volume in inner space
leaving the notes ring.

THE UNEXPECTED LESSON

Red leaves in my hands. The world is harder now;
the ladder I let fall so long ago
has rotted under straw, the open roof
admitted smoking rains, the raging equinox.

White horses of rain streaming through dark woods.
Today the little boy and little girl
he invented as a solitary friend
have taken shelter in my broken moods

and look out from a flawed highrise city
at detonative traffic, red plane trees,
and I remember a white handkerchief
with blue initials in the boy's pocket,

a square of mist or a blindfold
to keep me from things that I wouldn't see,
parental discord, a bird on the road
still shivering from an open red wound;

how was it possible that things should die?
How is it possible that they still do?
I'm still no nearer a resolution,
each year sees the foot try a thinner crust

above the seismic flaw. And nights are bad.
I find myself lost in a dream city,
the crowds stand pointing up at my parents
who kneel on a rooftop divided by

a dead flamingo fallen at their feet.
A jewel leaks from its eye. It seems to know.
Red leaves in my hands. The skies are flying low.
I break words open on a concrete street.

AS IT COMES

A green halo of sunlight through the trees.
The sadness bites watching the summer go;
a dusty lion slinks off through the town,
taking his gold mane South; the fast swallow's
triggered to leave.

I catch the light that works along my arm.
The poems written and the faces known
recede into the past. I'm taken back
to my first year out of school when I sat
above a valley and watched the stream fill
with red and gold leaves and wanted to stay
in that time and place indefinitely;
the afternoon light tigering the trees.

The cafés that I use for sitting out
and finding a poetry in the street,
keep a few tables tilted at the sun;
a red carnation in each water jar.

The things I found here were like counting stars,
the summer girls intersecting with inner space,
beauty that catches one out with the force
of falling down a flight of stairs.
Images that burst into flares . . .

And somewhere else that old valley of mine
will continue to fill with light and leaves.
The squirrels startle lovers; one by one
the chestnuts fall, cow-eyed and start to shine.

NEW AGE POETRY

It still goes on, the hope the century
will make it new: I read in Ashbery
the continuity, blue pieces picked up from the pot
surrealism aimed at the wall;
hands full of magic, Breton and Eluard,
Desnos's landscapes floating out of trance,
the poem sitting like a jaguar
on a roof in Montmartre, a tropical
forest blowing greenly across the sky.

The sudden explosion has moved elsewhere,
the ear listening to a volcano's mouth,
the eye that sees without its being there
have gone missing and energy's
translated underground; the singer's mike
fronting a fast band in a dark cellar.

We've been waiting too long for the event.
Post-Ashbery? and now the red leaves fall
on the sidewalk. If it's to happen soon
poetry needs the madness of the times
hyped to a fast energy stream,
a trajectory that goes through the wall
and into space.
                                    And do we have the tune?
We're looking for it in our orbital
scanning of what's new from a penthouse roof.
An era moving in like a wind-storm,
high pressure from the islands still looks promising.
If there's an aftermath, drag out a chair
and watch the debris float, and on the underside
of a banana leaf write the word truth.

PRESENTING EDGE

As the poplar leaf
shows white on its underside, a silver
twist away from the presenting
edge, so summer turns our lives

from the scarlet beanflower
to the loaded vine, waspish pear,
first chestnut leaves splashing the little square
in which the old sit reading,
watching the sky's presentiments.

The change over from day to day
is like moving towards a new country
by slow stages; the frontier guards
still lack a true identity;

their blurred uniforms are cut by red leaves.
Where are we going to and why?
Summer was long; its parched foreskin will burn

later by the cracked wall.
You'll turn round and age twenty years
closing the door on the sun-slatted hall.

FRENCH POETRY

Laburnum strings its yellow waterfall
into lilac. I read French poetry –
Sergalen, Breton, André du Bouchet,
the images more coloured than
a peacock's turquoise ocelli.
It's a parallel world they've created,
the one I shift to not by displacement,
but confirmation of reality.
A white sky like the inside of a shell
fluted with pink ribs forms an arch
in a rotunda overhead.
A girl wearing instead of a short skirt
a belt of scarlet roses highsteps by.
I'm closer to the image, a street scene
transformed into a tropical forest.
Hoopoes, jacaranda trees, violet suns.
I build cloud-sculptures, then I turn the page.
They're waiting behind black blankets with
                          cut-out eyes,
the brilliant ones who occupy the stage.

RETRO

It changes by the minute. What the poem meant
in its immediate touch-down, its first
surprised recognition in the mirror,
the language split-offs cooling on the page,
the shock at finding out the alien
had used my head and found this room
among so many in the universe,
and settled for the page, blindingly bright
on arrival in fast colours,
blues, emerald, scarlet, and later on
inviting me to drink, play a record
by way of celebration. A marriage
of days which cannot last a week
without multiple reproaches;

                                    I live

for the forward look, electrified nerves,
the pact with each new intruder,
the landscape I must duplicate, a beach,
a gold forest, cubist city, and entertain
this new love cautiously for fear
it disappears without a trace
out of my mind and into anonymity.

Reviving old affairs with poetry
creates imbalance, disillusionment.
The lipstick marks have been erased, a cool
settled over a fire that bit
ferociously like a first date
remembered by a time, a place,
and looked back on with astonishment
it ever happened, running now to meet
a different face, hoping I won't be late.

NIGHT STOCK

Once I was called from sleep by scented stock,
purple and white clusters flooding the dark:
I stood in moonlight converting the scent
into a childhood association
of passing quickly through gardens at night,
the sea behind me, and aware
between the terror I shouldn't be there,
and lights sunk into laurels, of a catch,
a fragrance to my fear, and years later
discovering that companion as stock.

Perhaps I went outside from delayed shock,
motivated by dream to conciliate
an old scar with the present. Hurried moths
were spotting on the air. I looked back in,
imagining a light around my bed
and that the sleeper dreamt the incident,
and that I'd wake to find myself assured
I hadn't moved.
                      I bent to inhale flowers,
the stock too potent for jasmine,
kneaded the damp grass with my hands and feet,
and went back in, confident I could claim
the brief living experience for mine.

NEEDLE'S EYE

I keep threading the needle's rusty eye,
pushing the line through
to the poem's end.
And then begin again.

Approximate, incomplete,
the work is circular
and not a radial star.

I know this way through and not the one back;
the camels wait at the oasis, blue
water-mirage in the air.

I lifeline words to the other.
My fingers show a line of blood
from the unsoftened vibrant point

on which an angel flares.

RETURN OF THE ALIENS

OTHER LAKES

When we arrived there, they were coming back
from the divide; the last hill farmer's truck –
a battered, obsolete amphibian
crowding up dust, the headlights two white moons
swimming into the broad-noon glare,
were alien, like a lunar landing-craft

encountering the wrong planet.
We'd seen the region on a film; the air
busy with scarlet dragonflies,
the igloo-shaped circular white houses
built round the crater of a central lake.
Sometimes, looking into the clear blue skies

they'd seen the lakes return, illusory
clouds of water, reflective mirages
eclipsing the hills, waiting to splash down
and become volume, density,
a dark-blue eye again. The commentary
showed an evacuated land,

a desiccated, sun-bleached exposure,
the crops burnt off, an aircraft left to rust
on the airstrip, and unnamed mustard birds
hardly distinguishable from the earth,
colonizing a parched basin.
We went, leaving our jobs, families behind,

the few of us embracing a future
where it seemed most impossible; charred trees,
ash flaking the atmosphere, dead locusts,

fist-heavy, blackened. We watched the truck go,
a lake circle, and stood beneath
the ovoid of its pulsating shadow.

ARCHIVAL

When we came back after the first time away
the earth had changed. We heard of ruins held
captive by the new military,
a diamond monolith raised from carbon;
a blonde woman who drove round in a car
all night, stopping to aerosol digits
on sites for potential landings.
But no one came after us to relieve

our shock, our disorientation;
the red dust glare that smudged the horizon.
We found a group of black matchstick children
conducting a judicial trial
over a dead US pilot.
Whatever the verdict he'd have no burial.
After we left they lit a fire.
Birds we had never seen before
flew over, big armour-plated grey birds
that might a century ago
have been our aircraft, bound for the desert.

In a building turned upside-down
I sifted through a bank's archives.
Wills, assets, vault deposits, names, the names
with which we'd once identified,
and just one suspect oddity – Skyray –
an interplanetary spy?
The blonde woman? We'd never know,

already we were building beneath a red sky.

THERE'S A PLACE

I need to get there. If the place exists
I have no map; the micro-continent
lives in my blood, disappears then returns
like an orbital comet. It's the promised land
I never reach, its pine forests resist
my inhaling resinous scent;
the little painted house above the beach
has a door open on unbroken sand.
The grottos mass with blue and yellow flowers;
a turtle meditates by the wave-line.
I call it Diamond Nebula;
a light within another light; a point
that's vanishing as soon as seen.

And yet at times the urgency
to get there is distracting. First hazel catkins,
the snowdrop's full-throated gold nectar drop,
tell me that now's the season to begin
the preparation, for the year will end
concurrently, we live so fast
in burning out our days. I make believe
I'll get there, and rest comes in thinking that,
so too a dynamic, to recreate
the vision, live with it:
                              I came this way.
I left footprints. The getting there is great.

TV GHOST

Their love scene's caught in an aquarium,
the TV washes it in blue and green
aquatic light – a motel in Kansas?
The blinds drawn on the buzz of nightbound cars.
He shifts station, and they are there, the stars
from earlier decades in black and white
muted contrasts, the living and the dead
snapping across his random choice,
facelifted physiognomies, the Hollywood
tableau, or nearer blood
splashed to red sea-anemones on the wall.

His world's contracted to this dimension;
a rectangular frame – the action's fast,
and there is always company,
an incoherent dialogue for the lonely.
Sometimes he goes outside and checks the hall
for a psychopath waiting with a gun.
There's something out there in the dark. The tube
projects a ghost, an isotope?
He leaves it money, car-keys and his watch,
but they remain untouched. The thing's implacable.
He can't narrow the haunting to a face,
a show: it might be John F. Kennedy
in the assassination shot, or else Monroe
come back for disembodied sex.
He watches all night and he sleeps by day.
He knows it must be Marilyn. Placed in his lap
on waking is a black, scented négligé.

SQUARE CLOUDS

A square black cloud looks like a building block
which will not fit the skyline. And a red
follows in quick succession. Twice a day
they come over like foundations
to a construction somewhere in the sky.
A space-mesa going up? It's not wind
floats them, but an autonomy,
they're flighted for somewhere and at high speed.
We watch them go; and later skeins
of orioles and storks go in pursuit,
much lower, observable by markings.

We live in drought, longing for the bright rains
that natural clouds might bring. Up on the roof,
a secretary in a bikini
takes instructions from a car-phone. The voice
is mobile anywhere. She focuses
on a red then a blue, lagging stragglers,
clouds going somewhere she can only think
and follow to the brink.
Perhaps we are nascent evacuees
who'll get there one day, and in our own time
and way, she tells herself, unhooking her gold bra
to let the sun in. She wants nudity,
it's like that when the block clouds pack over,
the atmosphere turns aphrodisiac.
She sees the blue one exit jerkily,
and takes the sun ten minutes on her back.

WAITING

They sit and wait by the receding lake,
a black-haired girl, a leather-moulded boy;
a brilliant litter of cans
scum at their feet. Advertising logos
eroded, red scrolls on silver –
the typeface flourishes that hit our need.

The drought's become a permanence,
the pleasure dinghies have been turned face down,
their blue and white paint flakes.
The couple look out into the blue day;
their minds tracking a radio's
instant street-poetry; the pop
that gives expression to the self-evident things
we see and do.
To them it is oracular.

They don't know if the world is burning up
into a dust crater; white dust a wind
will carry as a plume of smoke
across the world. A spiral tower
pointing to changes not an end.

They sit and listen and discourse like that.
He cracks a beer can open and they drink.
Others have come down to the shore.
They stand looking out, searching for a cloud
that might be white or red, or black or pink.

WHITE DOOR

They come through a white door into the world
and can't ever adjust again
to linear perspective.
They are full of space, and we the April rain
as it falls on grey lilac. They touch down
into dimensions which disorientate.
And Billy was a car salesman and John
a holistic healer, Ed a DJ
on an all-night station. The others drift
outside in independent orbits or retreat
into the inner in outer,
and John tries to tap me on the shoulder:
'we didn't want to come back from our place
outside time, you've grown old' he says,
'each new year adds a century to you,
although you miss the acceleration.'
And rain falls on the lilac; the white house
on the High Street has been deserted for so long
I can't remember it was occupied.
Was it a president lived there? No one
comes by this way, just a helicopter
with powdered rations. 'You were left behind',
Ed says, and Billy, 'there are others too
we visit.' Someone has a radio,
and by a freak occurrence picks up Ed's
old programmes. 1984
devoted to David Bowie? This time
I feel John's touch locate nerves in my spine.
The rain continues. And there's no white door.

THE SCRATCH

A waist and under-legs support: he carries her
in a wind-snatched white cotton dress the length
of a flat roof. She's unconscious, her hair
streams into space and pink clouds blow over
in a taut line of advancing snow hares.
No one looks up, the undemotic day
is purely functional, and zones of air
are being marketed, cerulean,
chemical-free – a summit house
right in the clouds. He carries her body
into the penthouse suite. The funeral
of the first earthed extraterrestrial
is being shown on the silent TV.
A silver car carries a rocket-shaped
coffin; four children dressed as harlequins
wait by the open grave. The time-separation
between the cortege and the cemetery
is dislocated by camera technique.
A mutant's banner proclaims Liberty,

Peace Between Planets. He cradles her head
and looks for the imperceptible scratch
between her eyes; the flaw that imitates
the one in the stratosphere. She comes round
and doesn't seem to see him, and a red
conical balloon comes lifting from the screen
in close-up. She is like a sleep-walker
balanced on a plank-bridge above a gorge.
She searches for her scar with a finger
and locates it. He shares that place of touch,
and watches her eyes change from brown to green.

LAYING IT DOWN

I'm looking for fast energy –
a poem doctored in a studio,
compressed, hard-hitting, firing on the nerves
with the contained tenacity
of life contracted to a record band . . .

Poetry's locked into parameters.
We need a voice that sees through a window
into a parallel future. A Picasso
creating art for the first time,
instating new worlds for the old.
A grammar of blue nudes. Let's get beyond
and into the unknown and reach the youth
of the 23rd century,
and find in language a new quality
that lifts the curtain as the wind might do
at the strategic moment that her breasts
flush rose, her dress folded over the chair,
and poetry looking in, free as air.

DISAPPEARING ACT

Where he lived remained an inveterate secret.
An X amongst so many apartments,
hotels – a rooftop level or back suite
looking out on flowering cherries
pinking the wind, or curtains drawn
all night, all day.
He lives there but he doesn't like to stay?
He fell to earth and can't acclimatize.

His blonde friend was discovered in a car
right out in the desert. He'd come to die
on the take-off point to the infinite.
No obstacle between him and the sky.
And there were so many who went that way

at the beginning. Was he real?
was the question most often on our lips.
We found a jacket once, a star
sewn in instead of a label.
His mauve lenses removed, revealed gold eyes.
If he was shooting film we never saw
the narratives we heard rumoured

about white lakes, a black hole clean through one
to some dimension.
We were never there.
One day we'd locate his physical space,
or find him running up steps to a house,
stone leopards watching as he disappears
into a place with no interior,
we following through into a garden,
searching the trees. And not a trace.

THE ORANGE DISASTER

An orange wall faces a black. Two white
are contrasting opposition. The one
who buys up Warhol's diamond-dust portraits
uses it as a studio.
He calls it an oriole facing snow.
His Bavarian visitors come twice a year
and talk of being Europe's rock-garden.
They bring him blue gentians and the digitally
remastered songs of Edith Piaf.
He flies his own flag. It is Klimt's *Danae*,
and on the other side a stars and stripes blue sky.
If he could instigate it, there would be
                                        black snow
falling from a green sky and oranges
suspended above the city,
dropped there and saved from a pulped disaster
by a trick of gravity.

He sleeps alone or between his two guests.
His inheritance never fails,
it's like pure water leaping through a rock
to sparkle. He goes with the flow.
The world outside has let him down.
It's too predictable. Rather he would have
                                        orioles
drumming at his window and red summits
surround the neighbourhood. But it is dawn.
His friends are sleeping. He gets up to think,
and fills his studio like that.
He peels an orange, wears a clown's black hat.

TRANS-ELEVATION

She thinks curled up in leopard skin. It's right
his face and hands are silver and they sit
in a glass rectangle, one side shaded
the others open to the street. The park's
sub-tropical; its rubber trees
point to occasional clouds, white and red
vaporous cubes. Her glass table's
a prism on which she places seashells,
starfish – a beach by Yves Tanguy
contributes to the notion of mental space.

They talk about the deepening.
They've changed like the environment; no cars
just helicopters and their sex
has part mutated. When she takes it in
it's through the ear, fragile helix
evolved to an aperture.
They've ceased to think of the future
because they've gone beyond it and look back
at photographs of the old world. That's her
as someone else; that's him in drag
when it was necessary.
London, circa 1980, and both
taken by a friend beneath a plane tree.

ECHO CHAMBER

Clouds swim inside the pool like fish. Dolphins
brushing the surface of a glass oval
that's emerald; the underwater floor
reflects images of contemporaries –
Warhol and Jagger, Bowie's face
appearing from a silver space
that's central to the montage. A black sphinx
keeps watch beneath a scarlet umbrella.
The human X-ray on the mirror door
is all you'll learn of the recluse who lives
inside the mansion. He is somewhere, lost

in looking for himself; his favourite ghost
instructs him in the studio
he's built to accommodate dictation
from weird electric frequencies. The screens
around his walls shout a print-out
of spiral flashes, impulse-dots, a shape
that's faceless, and he's come to call
Matisse's woman wearing a white dress.
Sometimes the echo-chamber filters sound
into the eight track pick-up; and he wears
a dress to match the painting. Invitees
to parties gather by the pool,
and look off at the dusty blue hill peaks
which are a physical reality
and not a painting. It is always day;
for five years they've lived without night,
the one inside and those gathered outside
amazed at the consistency of light.

THE UNANSWERABLES

Are always just beyond where thought connects
with a terminal. They are other there,
and warn by intimations, a mirror
catching the sun's angle between dark trees,
the possibility of a girl seen waving
from a hill, the white dust track around corn
leading to an abandoned car,
a mirage-figment when you go to touch
red bodywork and look for her.

And still they are our guides
although we never meet. They lead the way
like runners who have disappeared
out of sight of the field and grown into
imaginary participants.
I feel them on my nerves, shock-impulses,
the word beyond the word, the lightning flash
in its micro-second zigzag
seen out of the corner of the eye.
And still no thunder. Still a sky that's blue.

They have me over-reach. My limitations find
they are extensible, but every clear
leads to an impasse. I'm pulled up
against a blank and hear
their continuous departure. They have moved on
again, leaving me to approach
a point they left, was it ten years ago?
their travel is so fast.
I stop and start. My electricity
computes their messages. Today a red
car's parked for real beneath the same oak tree.

TELEPATHIC PEN-FRIEND

I write to you from the end of the world.

A single aspen shivers, and its leaves
are green-black hearts. Our house is white and square;
the back door opens on to air.
We hang a blue shark from the washing-line.

Sometimes we grow afraid. Supernovas
burn in the silence of deep space.
An angel makes a search across the beach,
crystal, supradimensional, alive
to possibilities of a landing?
We hide; knowing we have created him,
and later disowned our mental schema.
We've left an open grave beneath the tree

that fills with dead birds. On the shore
are starfish, gannets, a touch-down capsule
in which the astronauts were grilled.

We wait because there's nowhere else to go.
We've reached the edge, the end. But not to words.
Often I dream of a pen-friend
on the other side of the world. A map
of edges with a hole in the centre;
a correspondence by telepathy.

I know you're there across the frozen sea.

THE NEW AGE

We're in it, and it's caught us unawares;
the take-over was a premonition
that grew to a reality, a cloud-shadow
that never forecasted the sparkling shower
and how its silver bites back from the road.
How can I direct poetry
towards the future's disconnected images
that flash by on a filmic screen?
The word's gone underground. I heard it go
into the night guided by a gold star.
The swallows search for it, frisking the air
at dusk above this violet square.

The visual qualities pronounce themselves;
the superficial's surface-excess wins
by hooking our sensory need; that car,
that girl in leather with mauve sunglasses
are interchangeable with the movie
we've come out from, the stage-set is the same,
and music lifts us to a roof-garden;
the sequined guests look up as a helicopter
monitors the traffic canyons.
We're all in each other's film and conscious of that,
live through the imitative and not the real.
My words are a headless stem on a page;
I'm distracted by a red hat,
slashed jeans, a gold shoe, solarized faces,
the whole coloured accoutrement the poem wears
stepping into the imponderable age.

A NEW ORDER

We lived here in the question mark between
civilizations; a pinewood outback
purpling to fixed clouds, five red cubes
and two black triangles, or were they sculptures plinthed
on summits that we couldn't see?
We occupied the foreground; a city
built for inhabitants of a century
still in the making, each solarium
equipped with a sealed glass panel
marked Exit-Supply: the prepared capsules
for extinction, should it really happen.
And there were models seated in the empty rooms,
silicone structures with empty faces.
In time we gave them individualized features,
cosmetic masks, and spoke to them.
We'd come here as a small community
and failed to multiply.
                                 We lived exposed
in glass rooms, and the video library
was freakish, for it seemed to indicate
the worst had happened, and we were alone
in the prestructured city. And beyond?
We didn't dare to penetrate
the forest density. We faced the other way,
confident the models would come alive,
and govern us, impart a new order
to we, who'd already learnt to survive.

JEANS

We're the new ones in our expressive myth.
We carry the future into the hills
and leave it as an exhibit,
an art object – a pair of jeans kitted
with functional utilities,
a condom wallet, Walkman and cassette,
keys, dollar bills, an address book,
all the ephemera that fit
four blue pockets, additions to the legs.
We hook it to a barbed-wire tree
and leave the blue to bleach. It never rains.
Our artefact is taken in each time
new developments in technology
delete the contents. When a man took down
the denim-god and changed into the jeans,
and ran, they shot him from the air
and blood splashed on the worn blue cloth.
We re-instated our totem,
and set up guards and lost the liberty
intended by the patched logo.
It is a try-out stage. We need the thing.
We are the new race and we take it slow,
and plant out barbed-wire orchards on wasteground,
tend to our denims and sometimes we sing.

STATE BURIAL

They stay composed around the missing zoo,
twenty flamingos staring pensively
into a cultivated pool.
Behind them a city built of mirrors
reflects the uniform silver and blue
helicopter traffic. The President
stands leaning on a balcony;
her turquoise skirt shimmers like a peacock,
her bodyguard tells how the arid view
was once a Middle East city
before the interzoning changed. He keeps
one eye on the closed-circuit screen,

and one on the two pythons torpidly
withdrawn into a blank. His leotard
is black leather. He switches on the sun,
the artificial one in their own planetary
system, and then the daylight stars
which flicker brightly above the city.
Today is a State burial;
the President's mother will go to the freezer
to join the other incorruptibles
in ice. The sun will be black for two hours,
the airways closed. A draped helicopter
cortege will convey her body. Black panthers,
black flowers, black champagne.

She comes inside; news of the Square continent
marching against the Round is telexed through.
Events can wait. Her bodyguard lays out
black bra, black stockings, a black leather skirt,

a black wig, false black fingernails.
It's almost time. Under one eye,
he glues a tear, then selects a cassette.
He thinks of the flamingos. Soon they'll fly.

RECEIVERS

We came by day to an unknown city;
the rusting cars depressed outside of town
to a metallic carapace,
our guide a leopardskin cat-suited blonde,
brushing her hair back, pointing to a balcony
with its upright microphone and sten-gun
indicating a dictator?
a last speech before evacuation,
tanks or UFOs coming out of the sun?

We'd arrived from our own deserted town,
three of us big with the discovery
of absolute silence, and pushed the car
across white roads and found a blonde hitching
towards the signposted city. 'You are
the ones,' she said, and untabbed a coke can,
and settled back, authoritarian,
already an instructor . . .

                             No one here;
dehydrated flowers from a carnival
scattered over the streets, a zigzag trail
of someone's footsteps caked in blood.
Two mannequins standing on a pavement
outside a store, wine glasses stood
on a street table, red stains on white cloth.

We stopped and went inside a restaurant,
as though it was an ordinary day,
four of us unfolding our serviettes,
silent, almost expecting a waiter
to come from the partition with a tray,
and opposite us, seen through the window,
the mounted sten-gun's shadow on the street.

NEW DIMENSION

All the way round the coast they sang of how
the New Dimension activated hope,
sun-roofs open on sports models, they drove
past empty beaches, stopping once to sight
a school of whales surfaced on the skyline,
each balancing an orange sun, and right
the way to Blue Cube, Zen Heights, Red Berry,
they were sustained and the car stereo
supported optimism; the new ones
would meet with the discovery
of altered visual states: jewelled pine forests,
transparent mountains, lakes so clear
the eye can detect markings in a stone
500 metres down on a dark bed,
and there were other expectations: deer
and birds might be interpreted instead
of heard, and they would meet the X-ray squad,
the ones who saw through everything
without ever being seen; they would know
of their presence by the healing
that took place unawares. The colour men
were those who painted the landscape
in advance of those who came – a blue road,
improvised props, a landscaped house
that changed from white to pink to indigo.
They went in search of the new land and left behind
families, jobs, an old culture.
We watched them go. Mist in the redwood trees.
A light over the coast; a white dust cloud
dispersing with them into the future.

MODERN DAY

They've left their towels, an orange and a blue,
as rectangular inserts in the beach,
two opaque windows in a white hotel,

and gone off towards the stone jetty's arm,
which lacks the horizontal for an L.
They're strangers here and stay at the hotel
above the bay. Green ivy on granite.

It is an unfillably modern day;
the world is somewhere happening behind
the bluely improvised skyline;
nearer pink marker-floats, a tidal flag.

They know it's all beginning in a place
they've never been to, and the generous parts
are distributed to the random ones.
A man replaces a gold telephone . . .

They walk towards the crystal pane of air,
his hand rests on her bikini bottom,
slung low, two black triangles on a string.

They're waiting for the day to come alive.
They too can feel the changes, start to run,
as though by doing that they will arrive.

ENDLESS PURSUIT

The sharpened air, the leaf's scarlet canoe,
and higher great fleets of unsettled cloud
awake in me the need to find again
that one face in a street or bar
who's likewise crossed so many inner states
in search of finding the potential one,
smoking, writing, or sitting in a car
waiting for nightfall,

                               and the brilliant star

over the city pointing clear.

I say aloud the names of men I'd like to meet,
Rimbaud, Trakl, Artaud, Hart Crane,
half believing they've never died,
and are around and could be in this street
at a loose-end or in a cinema
watching Wim Wenders's *Wings of Desire*.

A vagrant on a building-site has lit a fire,
and tented himself in a black greatcoat.
It could be Artaud, a red snake
escaping from his sleeve?

I settle for whisky in a café,
and watch blue wreaths of mist smoke through plane trees.
My eyes anticipate someone,
lifting from the page with each new entry,
to drop again to print, alert, hopeful
they'll look in and decide to stay.

GETTING THROUGH

Today I'd like to meet André Breton
at a street café and to carry there
my blue thoughts in a vase, my red
as scarlet carnations, my white
as the invisible

X and Y chromosomes which define sex.
I wish the imaginative were alive
to contradict the commonplace
film in which we participate. My bed
floats above black waters all night.
A diver's down there directing a light
at paintings; I hallucinate
their colours; they are the sunset
I see on waking.
                    Pink burning red-blue.

Today I dream the anarchic poet is there,
his green ink writing in and writing out,
the wind blowing a woman's hair
from a black shell to a fly-away swathe.
He writes and watches, looking out for me,

and gold lions march down the century.